How to SLAY a DRAGON

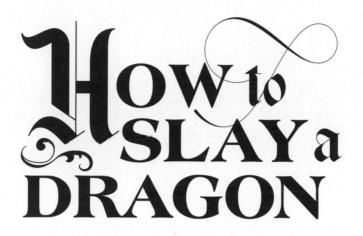

How to SLAY a DRAGON

A FANTASY HERO'S GUIDE *to the* REAL MIDDLE AGES

Cait Stevenson

TILLER PRESS

NEW YORK LONDON TORONTO SYDNEY NEW DELHI

An Imprint of Simon & Schuster, Inc.
1230 Avenue of the Americas
New York, NY 10020

First Tiller Press hardcover edition August 2021

TILLER PRESS and colophon are registered trademarks of Simon & Schuster, Inc.

For information about special discounts for bulk purchases, please contact
Simon & Schuster Special Sales at 1-866-506-1949 or business@simonandschuster.com.

The Simon & Schuster Speakers Bureau can bring authors to your live event.
For more information or to book an event, contact the Simon & Schuster Speakers
Bureau at 1-866-248-3049 or visit our website at www.simonspeakers.com.

Interior design by Jennifer Chung
Illustrations by Bruno Solís
Floral art borders by Vecteezy.com

Manufactured in the United States of America

1   3   5   7   9   10   8   6   4   2

Library of Congress Cataloging-in-Publication Data

Names: Stevenson, Caitlin, author.
Title: How to slay a dragon : a fantasy hero's guide to the real Middle Ages /
by Cait Stevenson. Description: First Tiller Press hardcover edition. | New York : Tiller
Press, 2021. | Includes bibliographical references. Identifiers: LCCN 2021003899 (print) |
LCCN 2021003900 (ebook) | ISBN 9781982164119 (hardcover) | ISBN 9781982164133
(ebook) Subjects: LCSH: Civilization, Medieval. | Middle Ages. | Quests (Expeditions)
Classification: LCC CB353 .S747 2021 (print) | LCC CB353 (ebook) | DDC 909.07—dc23
LC record available at https://lccn.loc.gov/2021003899
LC ebook record available at https://lccn.loc.gov/2021003900

ISBN 978-1-9821-6411-9
ISBN 978-1-9821-6413-3 (ebook)

For Dr. Mark Smith,
who knows that loving the past
means passing it on

CONTENTS

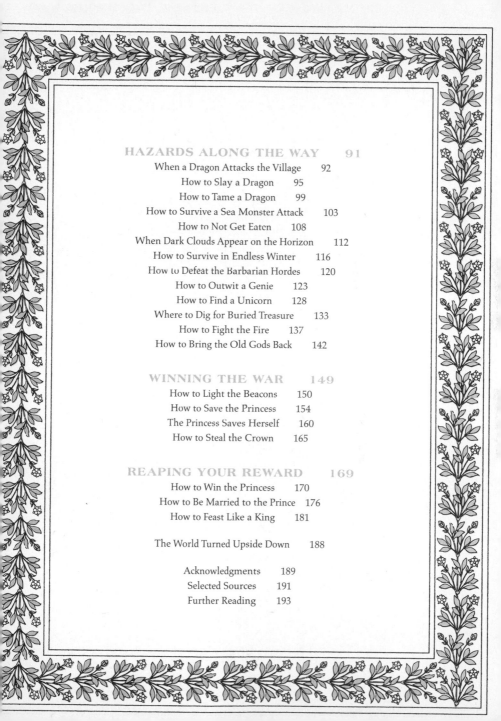

AUTHOR'S NOTE

ive years ago, someone asked me whether medieval rulers ever made plans for dealing with a dragon attacking their castle. I offered a few generic lines about the Dark Ages not actually being dark, and people knowing perfectly well that dragons are myth. But where's the passion in that answer, where's the imagination, where's the *history*? How does it lead you into another world that's also our own? Instead, I should have woven answers about how people dealt with fires racing from rooftop to rooftop in the Cairo slums, or imagined Londoners trying to fight air pollution. I've spent the past five years regretting my response that day. *How to Slay a Dragon* is my work of penance.

In my subtitle, I call the period that we're discussing the "Real Middle Ages"; this is a history book, although just a wee bit nontraditional. The stories, facts, and what they say about the Middle Ages all come from peer-reviewed secondary scholarship or my own consultation of primary sources. There are very few footnotes. (On the plus side, there are also no endnotes, because endnotes were clearly invented by elf-demons with a grudge.) I've kept a running list of references to keep me honest. Many of the primary source quotations are mine, but lack of access to some original-language texts and my inability to read Arabic mean I've occasionally relied upon the efforts of other scholars. Their work is credited in a section at the end of the book.

In several chapters, my interpretation of some primary sources differs from that of current scholarship. I've tried to briefly justify my views in each case, but we can all be grateful that this book isn't the place for full-blown academic arguments.

I've been a contributor to AskHistorians, one of the world's largest and most successful public history forums (www.askhistorians.com), for five years (*what a coincidence*). Very rarely, I've borrowed ideas or even a few sentences from one of my earlier answers (writing as /u/sunagainstgold) in this book. Per Reddit's terms of service, I hold the copyright to all my AskHistorians writing.

In some cases, I've relied upon scholarship conventions, such as the use of modern names for prominent figures (Charlemagne instead of Karolus Magnus) but the original forms for lesser-known ones (Katharina Tucher instead of Catherine). Non-Latin alphabets are transliterated (changed into our alphabet) without diacritical marks (for example, a instead of ā). Because medieval languages love you and want you to be happy, the name of one Slovak bandit family can be written as Glowaty or Hlavaty—they're still the same people who took the same town hostage. In cases like these, I've kept to one spelling throughout.

In other entries, I've trampled over scholarly conventions in ways that will leave other medievalists curled up in agony. Most notably, this includes the use of modern place names unless absolutely necessary. (Also, the Middle Ages ended in the 1520s, and I am unassailably correct about this. *Unassailably*.)

All of this is to say that the Middle Ages are the best ages, and I've done my best to pass on my love to you.

CAPITULUM INFODUMPIUM

thousand years and a hemisphere. The medieval world had a thousand years and half the planet's worth of other people you could have been.

You could have been Margaretha Beutler. After her wealthy husband's untimely death, Beutler donated all her money to the poor and journeyed around southwest Germany for five years, funded by those who donated money to her instead of to the poor. During her travels, she was probably preaching—in an age when Christian women were not allowed to preach or teach religion in public. Until, that is, she was arrested in Marburg for being "an evil thief" and sentenced to death by drowning. Understandably, Beutler preferred to make some powerful friends who found her a spot in a monastery instead, after which she went on to lead several monasteries of her own.

Or you could have been Pietro Rombulo, the Arab-Italian merchant who moved to Ethiopia, started a family, became the king's ambassador to Italy (and possibly India), and befriended an Ethiopian-Italian servant and a bishop.

You could at *least* have been Buzurg Ibn Shahriyar, who was not a real person but was still a celebrity, known for writing a book that included all the incredible stories people told him about pirates and sea monsters and islands beyond the edge of the world.

Nope.

You're just . . . you. *You* get to live in this village fourteen miles from the nearest market "town" and 1,400 miles from a town that

doesn't need air quotes to merit the name. Everyone in your village gossips in terror-laced excitement about the apocalypse, but you just think bitterly that the apocalypse wouldn't even acknowledge the existence of your village.

So when a mysterious stranger rides into town just before sundown, covered in dust because only the main roads are paved, shouting and waving a codex, you're finally excited. Even better, that stranger is looking for you. (Of course they're looking for you. You're the hero of the tale.)

They grab a flickering torch in one hand and your arm in the other and start to drag you down your village's only street. You're scared, but you heroically rise to the challenge and go along.

Of course, you have to walk pretty far to find a private spot, since peasants in your region live in village hubs surrounded by farmland. Finally, the stranger spots some mud and spreads their cloak happily over it. As you both settle in, they hold the book out to you.

"Oh, I won't be able to understand this," you say.

The stranger shrugs. "That's all right. Not everyone is Benjamin of Tudela, the Jewish explorer who traveled from Spain to Arabia and told tales of street warfare in Italy. But this is still a book to guide heroes who are setting off to slay a dragon, steal the throne, and defeat a few hordes of supernaturally evil creatures along the way. It'll help to have some background about the outside world first, even if medieval peasants like you know far more about the wider world than the lack of a public education system would suggest." They pause. "Luckily, spelling isn't standardized yet, so at least there's no need for a pronunciation guide."

Incipit capitulum infodumpium

The medieval world was four things: round, big, incomplete, and a sea monster.

As to the first: yes, and people knew it.

As to the other three . . .

In terms both geographic and painfully metaphorical, the "medieval world" was a hydra swimming in the Mediterranean Sea, its arms curling around the three continents: Asia, Europe, and Africa.

As far as you (and medieval geographers) are concerned, "Asia, Africa, and Europe" mean the northern coast of Africa as it curves around the eastern side to the south; the Arabian Peninsula and the lands to its north; western Russia north to Scandinavia; and then west across Europe to England at the farthest corner of the map. Iceland lay even farther out, beyond which was only the fearsome outer ocean. And also, cannibals.

In the reality denied by so many maps, the thinnest arms of the hydra reached even farther. They clung to the nexus (Latin unfairly fails to make the plural "nexi") of travel networks surrounding the West African kingdoms, the Swahili city-states, India, and China. Thule traders from northern Canada trekked to Greenland and traded clayware; Norse Icelanders sailed to the southern Canadian coast and brought home butternut squash. In short, the medieval world was a big place.

As a proper hero of a proper high-fantasy quest, your journey will take you to the outer ocean or even to southern lands so hot that the sun sets the ground on fire. Nevertheless, the thriving cultures beyond the Africa, Asia, and Europe you already know aren't part of the "medieval world" in the same way—their cultural and political shifts can't be forced into the same divisions of Antiquity and the Middle Ages.

As with every historical era, the Middle Ages have no definitive beginning or end, just sets of possible dates whose uniting characteristic is angering everyone who prefers different dates. Because you're a hero and you don't play by the rules, the dates that guide your thinking aren't the traditional ones, which are a starting date of 476, when the city of Rome was sacked by barbarians yet again, and an ending date of 1453, when England and France finally got tired of fighting each other. Instead, you're inclined to note that an invasion of one city does not precipitate the fall of an empire. After all, defining the end of an era based on the politics of the farthest corner of the world changes nothing for the lives of individual people.

For you, the Middle Ages are bounded by two revolutionary events that remade the map of the world in seemingly impossible ways. In the mid-seventh century, the birth of a new religion in Arabia and the zeal of its early believers drove the Arab conquest of the Near East and North Africa into southern Iberia. In the 1520s, the accidental birth of a new version of Christianity in western Europe shattered the world's greatest and most enduring power (that would be the power formerly known as *the* Church).

The medieval millennium did witness two attempts to remake parts of the geopolitical map. In a successful but rather unimpressive endeavor, the Christian kingdoms of northern Iberia spent nearly five hundred years attempting to become the sole rulers of the whole peninsula. The kingdoms claimed it was an act of *re*-conquest, despite the facts that, first, the Christians who'd ruled southern Iberia until 711 were, in their eyes, heretics, and second, the Christian kingdoms spent most of their time fighting one another.

In the . . . less successful attempt to redraw the world, assorted Christian kingdoms of western Europe attempted to conquer a swath of the Near East. The First Crusade (1095–99), as it became known, worked more or less as intended. Then Muslims spent the next 150 years or so kicking the western Christians right back out. The Second, Third, Fourth, Fifth, Sixth, Seventh, Eighth, and Ninth Crusades failed both to repeat the success of the First and to convince western Europe of the irony of their battle cry, *Deus vult* ("God wills it"). It's a little hard to label a Crusade successful when the entire crusader army is taken prisoner and when it requires one-third of France's annual revenue to ransom the king alone. Harder still to ignore a Crusade in which the same king led his army as far as Tunisia and promptly died of horrific diarrhea.

(Eastern Orthodox Christians, meanwhile, did have some temporary success recapturing their old territory, but does anyone ever think of them? Not really. Does this book do any better with that? Also not really.)

The story of the Middle Ages that you now look to for guidance is also the story of people trying to remake the "Christian world" and "dar al-Islam" from the inside. Some would point out that, over the course of the Middle Ages, these changes included massive population growth; the rebirth and rise of cities; technological development; in western Europe, the Church's ascension to a pretty spectacular amount of power; the rise of persecution based on religion and race; and other tidbits for trivia night. And as for politics . . . over the course of the Middle Ages, there were, in chronological and occasionally overlapping order:

- the Burgundians
- the Kingdom of the Burgundians
- the Kingdom of Burgundy
- the Kingdom of Upper Burgundy and the Kingdom of Lower Burgundy
- the Kingdom of Arles, composed of the reunited Upper Burgundy and Lower Burgundy
- the Duchy of Burgundy
- the County of Burgundy

And that's to say nothing of the part when the Kingdom of Lower Burgundy was also the Kingdom of Provence, except Provence was ruled by a count (who *was* also a king, just of Italy).

tl;dr: The "Medieval World"
- is very big, but doesn't truly encompass the entire globe or all the people in it;
- is mostly Christian kingdoms north of the Mediterranean;

- is mostly Muslim kingdoms in North Africa and the Near East;
- has the also-Christian Byzantine Empire squished between Islamic and western Christian territory in Anatolia, but most people don't care;
- more or less ended in the 1520s; and
- when Christians and Muslims went to war, the only thing "Deus" actually "vults" was for the French king to die of dysentery.

The People You Can't Wait to Meet

Medieval people were, first and foremost, people. They curled up with their dogs at night in thirteenth-century Egypt, and they drew up lists of good dog names in fourteenth-century England. They cheated; they lied; they loved their kids; they knowingly gave their lives to nurse and comfort plague victims.

They were also people who followed different religions or different forms of the same religion. In general, medieval religion was less focused on lists of beliefs, and served more as the ether of the medieval world—a sort of invisible communications network that everyone knew existed, that people participated in to different extents, and that formed the backdrop or even the means to everyday actions that weren't *about* it.

In the medieval world, religion was perhaps the most important factor (besides gender) in determining a person's identity. Because, dear hero, whether you're Christian, Muslim, or Jewish, you've been raised with very wrong and largely insulting ideas of what those *other people* believe. (Even when they're your neighbors.) If you're Christian or Muslim, you'll need to know that Jews believe in a single God who is the creator of the universe. Judaism holds that Jews are God's chosen people, the nation of Israel; and they take the terms "people" and "nation" very seriously. There are no attempts to convert others to Judaism. It's a religion and a people united by ethnicity as much as by a shared, extensive set of religious laws. As a result, medieval Jews independently control no territory. They're splintered into different cities across Europe and the Near East. Europe spent the second half of the Middle Ages becoming increasingly obsessed with *order*—be it scientific, social, or political—and defined order by punishing disorder. For Jews in the Christian west, it meant forced conversion to Christianity, expulsion from their home city or country, or pogroms that could wipe out a city's entire Jewish population.

Which brings us to the religion that claimed for its own the Jews' God, claimed the Jews' Bible—even writing a sequel—and then promptly forgot the "Jews are God's chosen people" promise. Christianity as a medieval (and modern, for that matter) religion is unique in two ways. If you're Christian, you believe that the one God is simultaneously three: God the Father, God the Son, and God the Holy Spirit. God the Son became human as a Jewish Palestinian carpenter named Jesus, who was indeed a real person, founded a religious movement (you can guess which one), and allowed himself to be crucified in order to give humans a chance not to spend eternity in hell.

Christianity's second unique feature was a strong central power and hierarchy of officials: the Church. Yes, *the* Church, even though there were already multiple Churches well before the Middle Ages. The Church in the west, based in Rome, was a political power in its own right, and many of its officials were essentially lords. (Others, especially the priests who operated on the local level—like the one who visits your village—often had to work second jobs in order to eat.)

The centerpiece of medieval Christian religious life was its formal church service, called Mass, and the central ritual of the Mass was called the Eucharist. The Eucharist, you'll want to know, is a ritual meal consisting of wine and a thin wafer (in the west) or actual bread (in other Churches). The idea is to re-create the death of Christ (as Jesus was known almost exclusively through most of the Middle Ages) on the cross and to participate physically in the defeat of sin and death.

The third great religion of the Middle Ages, Islam, returned Christianity's favor to the Jews by claiming the Jews' and the Christians' God, demoting Jesus to an important prophet, and holding to a set of sacred scriptures that adapted some of the earlier stories and added plenty of new material. If you're Jewish or Christian, you'll want to know that Muslims believe God—Allah in Arabic—dictated their scripture, the Qur'an, to Muhammad (also a real person, who died in 632 CE), who founded Islam and remains its central Prophet or Messenger.

Medieval Muslims' day-to-day religious life revolved around praying, which they were encouraged to do five times a day and with a special emphasis on Friday. Wealthier Muslims, including women (who controlled their own money and property), often took their religious requirement of donating to charity very seriously. If you're Muslim, you'll dream of making the most important pilgrimage of them all, called the hajj. On the one hand, it was perfectly legitimate for people who couldn't afford the trip to Mecca to never make their hajj. On the other, you had people like *mansa* (king) Musa of Mali, who distributed so much gold to charity on his way through Egypt that he single-handedly crashed the Mediterranean economy for a decade.

Judaism, Islam, and Christianity were not the *only* religions in the medieval world. Berbers and the Sámi peoples in particular maintained their indigenous belief systems. Muslim writers often interpreted Hinduism and Zoroastrianism in terms of ancient Greek mythology. And Christians . . . well, Christians converted pagan kings and kingdoms to Christianity, then wrote down all surviving information about pagan religion, spun through the writers' propaganda machine.

Of course, geography alone won't tell you anyone's religion or skin color. The Islamic regions of Iberia were home to Muslims, Jews, and Christians; to Arabs, Berbers, blond-haired and blue-eyed Muslims, and at least one man who dyed his red hair black to fit in better. (So much for the Christian writers who described all Muslims as "black.") Thirteenth-century German artists, who had probably never left their hometowns, could carve sculptures of saints whose skin color and features made them look exactly

XXI

CAPITULUM INFODUMPIUM

like the people Arab merchants lived near in Islamic sub-Saharan Africa. Jewish merchants from Islamic Cairo joined in the Indian Ocean trade, and Greek Christian women married Muslim or shamanist Mongol khans.

And you probably don't need a geography lesson—or any guidance at all, really—to know that Christians (and very occasionally Muslims) could turn on their neighbors of other faiths with sudden, swift, bloody brutality. People, after all, are people.

tl;dr:
- Medieval people could be nice
- Medieval people could be pretty darn evil
- Dogs are cute

Explicit capitulum infodumpium

Finally, you can't take it anymore. You snatch the book out of the stranger's hands. "No!" you practically shout as you flip it open and slice your hand down toward the first page of text. "I know plenty about the world! I can't understand the *words*. I'm part of the 94 to 99.9 percent of the peasantry who can't read!"

"*Yet*," says the mysterious stranger, ignoring your tone. "You can't read *yet*. That's all right. I'll read it to you. How else will you learn how to undertake a heroic quest, have adventures, slay a dragon, defeat the forces of evil, and save the world?"

They take the book back and smooth down the first page reverently. The stars sparkle in the pure blackness above your head, unbounded by air or light pollution. Torchlight and shadows dance across the parchment as the stranger starts to read.

"Here begins . . ."

CAPITULUM INFODUMPIUM

Incipit Liber de Dominis Draconum

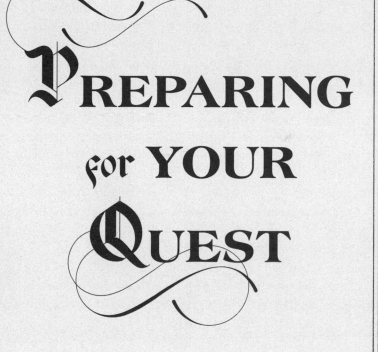

Preparing for Your Quest

HOW *to* FIND
the CHOSEN ONE

hen you were born, did it rain serpents? Did the sun rise in the west and set in the east? Did your mother casually let slip that your father was a demon in disguise?

Answer yes to any of the above? That's not good. The first rule of being a hero is that you don't want to be the chosen one. And those three were all signs of it.

Strictly speaking, being the chosen one in the Middle Ages didn't have to be bad. The three great religions of the medieval world around the Mediterranean—Islam, Judaism, and Christianity—all looked forward to God's chosen one, who would redeem them from suffering (which is a polite way to say viciously slaughter their enemies). In practice, however, the most popular chosen one by far was Christianity's favorite *anti*-messiah, the evil Antichrist, who was prophesied to be locked up by Alexander the Great behind the gates of Gog and Magog. The eventual defeat of the Amazons who guarded the gates would free him to unleash the apocalypse and the ruin of the world.

Ruining the world is not heroic.

But the second rule of being a hero is that you *are* the chosen one. Which means that the beginning of your quest revolves around two key questions: How will the forces of good or evil find you? And when they find you (because they will), can you fight fate as well as dragons? Three possible solutions present themselves.

A giant wheel burns in the sky, its outer rim made of fire and a thousand swords. The wheel is suspended from the heavens on thirteen chains, with only thirteen angels preventing its flames from lighting the earth on fire and annihilating all of humanity.

And then the whole sky is made of fire—fire that falls to the earth. Terrified people run to the deepest caves, but they find no hiding place down there. Only those who had heeded the earlier signs survive—and only if they never look back.

Is that the future you fought for?

If you don't want this vision to come to pass, it's a good time to start trusting divine revelations, even if they identify you as the chosen one. Medieval Christian women would certainly have hoped that you would.

The Church in the Middle Ages banned women from preaching and teaching religion in public. Starting in the twelfth century, however, some women figured out that they could do just that anyway if they convinced priests that God was speaking through them. Feeling left out, men consoled themselves by reasoning that if women were the physically and spiritually weaker sex (according to medieval medicine, which is famous for its accuracy), then of course God would find it easier to speak through them.

The chances of large- or even medium-scale success were tiny. But the women who did succeed often did so dramatically—both in terms of their visions and in what they did with their resulting authority. Abbess Hildegard of Bingen (1098–1179) became a celebrity throughout Europe as a composer, theologian, advice columnist, and apocalyptic prophet. Men wrote prophecies using her name in order to give them credibility. Mechthild of Magdeburg (d. 1292), who chose to forge her own form of religious life outside monastery walls, made Church leaders so angry that they threatened to burn her book—the first step toward burning *her*. Peasant and political activist Marie Robine (d. 1399), who saw visions of the burn-

3

ing wheel of a thousand swords, got quite rich and decided to live in a cemetery.

Of course, Hildegard's prophecies of the end of the world didn't come to pass. Mechthild's didn't come to pass. And somehow, Marie's burning wheel failed to fall from the sky, and humans failed to flee to caves.

But all that lack of apocalypse doesn't prove that you can't trust oracles and visions to identify the chosen one. It just means you have to choose the *right* one to find the right chosen one. In this case, that would be Elisabeth Achler von Reute.

Von Reute (1386–1420) was a religious sister and future saint, but that's not why you want to trust her prophecies. Your expectations should be based on the miracles she worked, which included locating a new well so her community wouldn't have to haul water all the way from the river in the dead of winter. And your evidence should be in the outcome: she correctly prophesied that the Great Schism tearing apart the western Church would end at a council in Constance.

Granted, her visions didn't tell her anything further. Granted, the only record of her prophecy was written down several years after the fact. Granted, it was recorded in a book that was 50 percent propaganda.

Still! Visions work.

At least, the ones that don't say anything useful.

♨ FATE AND FIGHTING IT #2: FORTUNE-TELLING

Swords, crystals, mirrors, the shoulder blades of sheep . . . perhaps you would gain more confidence in identifying the chosen one by looking closer to the (unburned) earth. The medieval world wasn't exactly hurting for surfaces on which to know the present and read the future. People lived in a universe where everything flowed out from God and was set in its terrestrial and cosmic place by God. To almost everyone, objects and living creatures pointed to the secrets of time just as smoothly as they did physics and chemistry.

There were always, of course, a few naysayers who thought trying to *discover* those secrets inevitably meant flirting with demonic powers. Unsurprisingly, people sought those secrets anyway, and people taught those secrets anyway.

The medieval elite were actively uninterested in preserving peasants' voices, so the folk traditions of palm reading, astrology, and divination are all but lost. Good thing those scholars did, however, record traditions that blended academic knowledge with the "popular" practices they grew up with.

And they recorded them in abundance.

Want to investigate the underlying natural processes that allow cow bones to display the outcomes of battles or how many women don't want to marry you? Don't care about why it works, but hoping for diagrams and tables that explain how to interpret your observations of the aforementioned skeletons? *Excellent.* You can look at the contents of books in Arabic, Hebrew, Latin, and medieval Greek; in books that originated in ancient Greece or Rome; and in books that claimed to originate in ancient Greece or Rome. And you definitely want to look at multiple books, because divinatory books liked to disagree.

In one untitled and anonymous book from around 1300, for example, you could read that men with small hands might seem nice initially, but will turn on you. Women with small hands, however, are uninterested in men and don't want to have sex. In one (also untitled and anonymous) contribution from the 1350s, you could learn that if one of the three major lines running across your palm ends at your ring finger, you will "die in water."

Or consider the lines that form a triangle between the outside edge of your palm, the space between your index finger and thumb, and more or less the base of your palm: If you're a hero, that triangle pretty much has to be equilateral—which means you're trustworthy and capable of becoming famous. If the top line is longer, you're a thief. Oh, and if any of the lines are "pale," then congratulations, you'll die on the gallows.

You'd better get some black ink and start drawing that triangle.

✿ FATE AND FIGHTING IT #3: ANCIENT VERSE

Go relax with a quart of beer at a fifteenth-century Nuremberg inn or with a barrel of wine at a thirteenth-century Cairo street party. When it comes to fulfilling ancient prophecies written in a forgotten codex, fate has already fought and lost.

If you're a medieval Muslim, the thought of ancient verse prophecies probably never even crossed your mind. Islam and its major prophet were born in the Middle Ages. To you, ancient verse is pagan poetry from the era before God's revelation, preserved so its Arabic can provide insight into interpreting the Qur'an.

If you're a medieval Jew, you're probably snickering at the Christians who believe some peasant in Galilee fulfilled *your* messianic prophecies— and snickering harder because no matter how often those Christians persecute your people for knowing they're wrong, Christians "somehow" never defeat God's chosen people.

If you're a medieval Christian, the nonbiblical "ancient" verses you're treating as prophecy stand a good chance of being very medieval, with authors who pretend their verses are older so readers will be more interested.

So, whether you've got divine messages, fortune-tellers, or ancient poems pointing to you as the chosen one of the medieval world, you can relax. Fate has already fought itself, and fate has lost.

But when you enjoy that quart of beer or barrel of wine, be sure it's weak enough to be an everyday drink. You might have figured out how not to be the chosen one, but you've still got a dragon to slay.

It's time to be your own kind of hero.

HOW *to* NOT
MARRY *the* PRINCE

o, you're off to slay a dragon, steal a throne, and maybe end a reign of evil or two. But would you also like to turn sheep into locusts? How about being smarter than the fifty best scholars in the world? Maybe you'd just like to kill your abusive father with lightning.

If so, it might help to look to the examples of extra-holy religious women. It's true that Margaret of Antioch, Barbara of Nicomedia, and Katherine of Alexandria were all brutally tortured and murdered, but they also were not real people. Nevertheless, medieval Christians cherished the legends of these "virgin martyrs," because they knew one thing above all: if you're going to be a hero(ine), you can't marry the prince.

English noblewoman Christina of Markyate, who was a real person and lived from about 1096 to 1155, certainly knew it. She was a teenager when the bishop of Durham (who couldn't marry) sought to make her his concubine. Afraid she wouldn't be able to fend him off physically, she locked him inside the room where he "proposed" and then fled. It didn't stop her parents and the spurned bishop from betrothing her to a nobleman closer to her own age. With no choice but to escape, Christina hid behind a tapestry, clinging to a nail on the wall so her feet wouldn't be noticed as her husband-to-be and his conspirators searched the room by torchlight. She was well prepared—she had time to flee through another door, jump out a window, scale a fence, and *run*. At that point, there was nothing to be done except find her own conspirators, put on men's clothing, and ride as fast as she could to a hermitage.

Oh, and then defeat an infestation of toads by singing religious songs.

It's a tad unrealistic, yes. (What gave it away—the toads?) This lone record of Christina's early life is called a hagiography—designed to shape the details of the subject's biography to signal their holiness to a Christian audience. Christina's adventures may or may not have happened, but they were "authentic" to their readers, telling the audience that she was a saint the same way that the presence of armor, mud, and Vikings tell you it's the Middle Ages.

Now, the chroniclers of Fatimid power broker Sitt al-Mulk needed no such religious motivation to tell her story.

This behind-the-scenes "adviser" was born in the Fatimid dynasty's abandoned Tunisian capital and lived out her life in its thriving Cairo headquarters. Sitt al-Mulk had brains from birth and gained political savvy from her adolescence at court as the caliph's granddaughter. After all, what's early medieval politics without some power struggles? (Nothing. Sometimes literally.)

As a young woman, Sitt al-Mulk played her suitors against one another. She expertly elevated her family's position and power while building up her own political networks. To be clear, those networks included a large military division, as well as enslaved advisers who acquired vast wealth and power of their own. In 995, her brother al-Hakim inherited the throne at age ten, while his chief advisor-general Barjawan inherited the real throne in his capacity as regent.

Sitt al-Mulk prudently used this time to continue not to marry, to acquire more allies, and to ply her brother with extravagant gifts. So when one of those allies assassinated Barjawan (who knows why?) in 1000, al-Hakim was ready to listen to his sister. The result? Cairene cultural life flourished, and the Fatimids' international profile grew dramatically.

During the next seventeen years, say the chroniclers, Sitt al-Mulk was responsible for the caliph's *good* internal decisions, which helped maintain the loyalty of far-flung provinces. Because her own allies carried out many of those orders, it's rather likely that Sitt al-Mulk was involved in these decisions. Another sign of her influence? Negligent leaders like the ruler of Tinnis, a wealthy city near Alexandria, paid their royal taxes and tributes . . . to Sitt al-Mulk's private coffers.

Al-Hakim didn't enjoy playing second fiddle to his sister (maybe one of the reasons he later banned music). In the dangerous world of the Fatimid court, his primary methods of disproving his own impotence were (1) assassinating his sister's high-ranking supporters, and (2) making financially and politically disastrous decisions. (To be fair, it's hard to make wise choices when a large number of people think you're divine, and you may or may not agree with their assessment.) These choices included designating two heirs in 1013, neither of whom were his sons, and attempting to assassinate his own children and their mothers. He also exercised his possible godhood by forbidding women to leave their homes, seizing the property of the Coptic Christians who had been among his biggest supporters, and banning music and wine. Which made him exactly as popular as you would think.

In 1021, al-Hakim disappeared.

Sitt al-Mulk took the lead in accusing one of her brother's enemies of being his murderer. She also led a coup d'etat, assassinated one of al-Hakim's chosen heirs and exiled the other, declared one of her underage nephews the true heir, and claimed the role of regent for herself. Princes need not apply.

But Sitt al-Mulk was a Fatimid princess, you say. *Christina of Markyate was a saint. They found ways not to marry, but they aren't me. I could never be them.* Well, consider this: Around 1200, men who write hagiographies of women saints will start adding a disclaimer for their readers and listeners—a change from how they were supposed to understand earlier hagiographies. She, they say, should be admired, not imitated.

Christina's hagiography was most likely written somewhere around the middle of the 1100s. In other words, you don't have to *be* a princess or a saint to spurn marriage and be a hero. Imitate away.

HOW *to* FIND YOUR MENTOR

hat hero ever saved the world without a mentor to learn from, surpass, and watch die in a noble self-sacrifice to convince the hero to stand on their own? You already know what you're looking for. Old guy, white beard. Tall, pointy hat (some of the time). Robes, of the scholarly sort. Pretty good with magic. Also, son of a demon and buried alive in a rock.

Maybe you don't want Merlin after all.

Fortunately, the Middle Ages still provide two large groups of people who are eager to be your mentor, even if you aren't a legendary British king named Arthur and you didn't inherit a mentor who brought about your birth by disguising your father as your stepfather in order to rape your mother. (Merlin's résumé: the gift that keeps on giving.) You've still got saints, and you've still got teachers. All you have to decide is which category you prefer, and you're all set for your mentor to find and choose you.

So sit back, relax, and listen to the saints and the teachers argue their cases for why they will do the best job nurturing you and guiding you to success on your specific quest.

❀ CONTESTANT #1: SAINTS

The natural, logical choice for a mentor in the Middle Ages is a saint.

Christian saints were the one-stop mentor shop of late medieval Europe. They were eager to help out, there were so many of them that even the Church couldn't keep track, and you could trust that they wouldn't turn out to be secretly evil. Most important for heroes, they could do the impossible. Saints were supernatural microphones. People could call on saints to feel closer to a God who was already everywhere. Saints would make sure that God answered the prayers of Christians who asked them to intercede, even though God only does what God wants.

In other words, saints can show you how to obey God's commands, survive a battle, win a battle, heal the sick and suffering, help your dead relatives go to heaven, and ensure *you* go to heaven (but not quite yet). And, of course, they can show you how to rain death and destruction upon your enemies. All you have to do is pick a saint or two and follow their example of how to lead a pious life.

Straightforward and exciting enough for a hero, right? Just take, for example, Katherine of Alexandria. (Never mind that she wasn't a real person. Her legend made her real in the ways that mattered, just like Margaret of Antioch and Barbara of Nicomedia.) Katherine was a third-century pagan (!) princess, exceptionally smart, beautiful, and charismatic. She absorbed all the education she could get; her father was impressed enough to build an entire library for her. Upon his death, she inherited the kingdom at age fourteen. Everyone insisted that she get married so a proper man could rule. *Queen* Katherine laughed and insisted she was quite suited for the task herself, thank you very much. And she was.

Katherine was a scholar, teacher, and wise ruler even before converting to Christianity, so you can be confident that the skills were hers alone. You can also be sure that she's willing to be your mentor. As queen, she taught her subjects the basics of Christianity and then led them to conversion by example. More impressive, when the still-pagan emperor of Rome visited, she stormed up to him and ordered him to stop executing Christians. He snorted and said the equivalent of "Shut up, little girl." Queen Katherine responded with the equivalent of something even ruder, and then used her knowledge and wit to prove he was a terrible ruler.

The last part was the most spectacular. Fifty pagan scholars challenged

11

her to a debate over religion—fifty, at the same time. Eighteen-year-old Katherine's rhetorical brilliance and knowledge of ancient Greek philosophy (really) turned them into mewling balls of shame.

(Another highlight? Katherine is arrested and tortured horribly for being Christian, but the torture device explodes and kills four thousand other people. Of course, the emperor had to have Katherine killed straightforwardly after that; she wouldn't be a virgin martyr if he hadn't. And then she wouldn't be a saint, and you wouldn't have her to guide you.)

The life of Katherine is a great story with a great heroine, and medieval Christians loved it. Fifteenth-century Nuremberg writer Katharina Tucher named her daughter Katrei, chose the monastery of St. Katherine as her retirement home, and eagerly read the biography of her fellow namesake Catherine of Siena (a real person). Heck, 50 percent of the infamous King Henry VIII's wives were named Katherine!

The thing is, most Christians besides priests and nuns and Tucher were illiterate and couldn't read Katherine's story for themselves, so they only heard the Church's version of how to imitate her. Which was, essentially, don't have sex, be happy about suffering, and don't have sex.

Bet you weren't expecting *that* to be the takeaway from a story about a teenage girl who loved to read, argue, and tell kings to go shove it.

So, in the end, maybe just scrap the idea of a saint as your mentor altogether. Because consider this: half of Henry VIII's wives were named Katherine, but so were half of his executed wives.

❦ CONTESTANT #2: TEACHERS

The natural, logical choice for a mentor is obviously your favorite teacher. Just do it. Embrace the cliché. After all, that's what all the students around you are doing. (Of course, all the students are male, teenage, Christian, somewhat wealthy, and literate in Latin, but who's counting?)

Before the creation of the first universities around 1200, advanced students would trek across multiple countries to study with a specific teacher, wherever they had set up shop. (Universities basically happened when enough students and teachers were in one place that they banded together to demand special legal rights, such as not being charged by the city if they committed crimes.) So right away, you know that your potential mentor is willing to teach you, is very good at the thing you want to learn from them, and has enough experience in the role for their reputation to have reached even *your* village.

The only real downside to choosing a teacher in high medieval Europe was the competition among students to gain the potential mentor's special attention. But even then, you'll find inspiring cases of a teacher's students coming together to make real change in the world.

Case in point: John Scotus Eriugena (c. 815–c. 877), who started off as the top scholar in Ireland. Then he was personally invited to run the school at Aachen in western Germany—the best school in ninth-century Europe. Students flocked to study with him, and why not? (Never mind the rumors.) Eriugena was a brilliant theologian, philosopher, and translator. The perfect mentor. (So what if your friend heard from his brother, who heard from their cousin, that Eriugena had some flaws as a teacher?) Under Eriugena's leadership, the Aachen school somehow became even bigger and better. (In a thousand years, people will be confident they were just rumors.) Its glowing reputation grew even brighter. (Rumors are absolutely *no* basis for ruling out the idea of teachers as mentors. None!)

And sure enough, Eriugena's leadership and scholarship united students in a way never before seen in medieval Europe. Sometime in the late 870s, they banded together during a lecture one day and stabbed him to death. With their pens.

But they're just rumors, right?

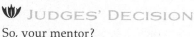 JUDGES' DECISION

So, your mentor?

Good luck.

HOW *to* TRAIN *a* WIZARD

learned necromancy in both kinds with the help of the art of these books," wrote John of Morigny (c. 1280–after 1323). "Similarly geomancy, pyromancy, hydromancy, aeromancy, chiromancy, and geonegia, and almost all their subdivisions." Perfect. There really were forms of magic in the Middle Ages, people did practice them, and, best of all, they learned how to do it from books.

Set aside the slight problem that you almost certainly cannot read, because peasant life doesn't require literacy skills all that often. John's books can be your road map, and John himself can be your guide. Even better, John was a devout Christian monk. (Don't worry—the heroically inevitable run-in with inquisitors always occurs later in a quest.)

Best of all, John *wants* to be your guide. He didn't just write spell books—which he did, and with gusto—he also wrote a semi-autobiography describing how he learned, worked, and taught magic. He's practically begging to be your guide.

Whether you can trust him is another matter.

There are three points to consider regarding trustworthiness. First, John tells the events out of chronological order—neatly disguising how the timeline of his supposed life story makes zero sense (unless he *really* hates his sister). Second, this purported autobiography reads suspiciously like an advertisement for why people should use his spell books instead of the popular ones. "Suspiciously like" in the sense that he says so outright. Third, as we will see, John taught himself magic in order to cheat on his homework.

According to John, he impressed his monastic superiors so much that they selected him to go study law at the university in Orleans, so he could represent Morigny Abbey to the outside world. (And as things turned out, represent it *while living in* the outside world, suggesting the other monks might have had a slightly different motivation for sending John to school.)

However, John promptly ran into several problems that should not have existed. First, he got interested in a book of spells and started to have demonic visions (which was apparently not a problem) but continued to convince himself that he was doing what God wanted (which was definitely a problem). Second, he was *bad* at magic, and so looked for help from an Italian Jew (a problem for historical accuracy, because a "Jewish sorcerer" leading a Christian to magical perdition was an odious and omnipresent literary trope). Third, he sought help for his difficulties with one book of magic from a *second* book of magic. This one—probably the most famous necromancer's manual of the Middle Ages—was called the *Ars notoria*, which more or less means "The Notary Art" but sounds much cooler in the original Latin. Fourth, John didn't want to attend class, so he did what any lazy student would do—namely, he taught himself to be a wizard. For real this time.

Jacob the insidious Jew from Lombardy had already pointed the way. Who needs a textbook or class when the *Ars notoria* promises overnight learning of any subject in the world?

So John set aside his law studies to learn the ritualistic prayers that would help him study law. Each night before bed, the monk who wanted so badly to be a wizard made a practice out of reciting one prayer laid out in the *Ars notoria*. He was subsequently visited by a wonderful dream from which he awoke with the knowledge that prayer had promised: necromancy, geomancy, pyromancy, hydromancy, aeromancy, chiromancy, and geonegia. Things every lawyer should know.

On seven of those nights, however, John was visited by visions he had not sought. In the first one, the shadow of a hand blocked out the moon, and then stretched out along the ground toward John. But the shadow evaporated as soon as the dreaming monk cried out for help. In the second, third, fourth, and subsequent visions, some sort of demonic or diabolical creature came closer and closer to pouncing on John, ensnaring him, and then suffocating him to death.

And herein lies one of John's key pieces of advice for wizards-in-training: If you pray for magical knowledge and the devil delivers it to you, it is *definitely* because your sorcery is so pleasing to God that the devil wants to interfere. Definitely.

You'll finally know it's time to stop for real after that vision in which an angel beats you up while Jesus gives you a disapproving glare.

And so, as John writes, his adventures with the *Ars notoria* came to a close. He was firmly convinced the book was diabolical and its prayers would lead him nowhere except to eternal perdition. From that point on, it was only good old-fashioned procrastination and cramming for him. (Except for the part where he retained all his knowledge of necromancy, geomancy, pyromancy, hydromancy, aeromancy, chiromancy, geonegia, and *maybe* law. John isn't clear about that last part.)

Well . . . he brought his *own* adventures with the *Ars notoria* to a close. But did I mention the part where he trains his little sister to become a wizard?

John was a teacher at heart, you see. The whole point of his autobiography was to promote his other writing, which was primarily beginner-level textbooks. He even mentions how, at one point, he had started writing his own instruction manual for necromancy but threw it away when God convinced him it was bad.

So when his teenage sister Bridget wouldn't stop pestering him about teaching her to learn to read (a feeling you know all too well), John lovingly gave in. And, well, the *Ars notoria* had granted him such quick command over the powers of fire, water, earth, air, demons, and palm reading; what better book to use to teach her how to read? No, not via the spells in the book. The actual book. That old children's classic *A is for Ars, D is for Diabolus.*

Like her brother, Bridget was an eager learner and had no desire to stop with the alphabet. Unlike him, she used the *Ars notoria* to learn to (i) read, (ii) write, (iii) speak Latin, (iv) sing church songs, and (v) overcome stage fright. But the purity of her goals made no difference. Bridget likewise began to suffer horrific nighttime visions of the devil.

According to John, he knew instantly that the demons who drove the operation of the *Ars notoria* were tormenting his sister. He was equal parts terrified for her and angry at himself for leading her into a diabolical trap. John urged Bridget to swear to stop using the book of magic for any future learning, which she did. And from that day forward, she could read, write, speak Latin, sing church songs in public, and beat up demons whenever they came after her.

No, it doesn't make sense that John would use the *Ars notoria* himself, realize the book was diabolical, and then tell his beloved sister to use it. The other timeline of events makes no sense, either: John used the *Ars notoria*, told Bridget to use it, realized the book was diabolical, kept using it himself, and then gradually realized the book was evil.

But hey, whatever tale made people read his own books, right?

His books. Which were, in fact, beginner-level textbooks. Of magic.

So much for a simple autobiography. John's book teaches . . . various prayers and rituals that promise to unlock various forms of knowledge for its readers. Of course, because the title *Ars notoria* was already taken, John had to call his work the *Book of Flowers*.

His autobiographical introduction more than makes up for the less marketable title. The overarching story tells readers that the *Ars notoria* will corrupt them, and they shouldn't use it. His little anecdote about trying to write a necromancy manual but throwing it away starts to make sense, too. John threw that book away because God disapproved of it. If he didn't throw away the *Book of Flowers*, God clearly approved of it. In the guise of abject humility—confessing his own necromantic sins, lamenting about nearly damning his sister—John explains to the reader exactly why they should use *his* book to learn magic.

The medieval Church certainly saw past John's rhetoric. In 1323, the French clergy staged a major event in which they burned copies of the *Book of Flowers*. This was a direct threat to John's life. One way or another, he receded into the background after that date. Sources are silent on the rest of his life.

Oh, but the book. The *Book of Flowers* was copied again and again for the next hundred years. Scribes personalized the prayers in the book with their own names, or the names of the customers who had purchased the copies. People didn't just own or read the *Book of Flowers*. They used it. They taught themselves its prayers, spells, and rituals. They taught themselves its magic.

John of Morigny may or may not have actually taught himself sorcery. He may or may not have actually taught sorcery to his sister. But with all the copies of the book he wrote that the Church condemned as heretical? John and Satan did, in the end, train reader after reader how to be a wizard. Readers like you.

HOW *to* DRESS
for FIGHTING EVIL

ven the king of Sicily knew it: "Enemy powers are not repelled by pompous ornament, but rather through the necessary use of arms," said the law.[1]

That's kind of a bummer.

For one thing, it's incorrect. Enemy forces can also be repelled by sorcery, bribery, or a cop-out deus ex machina. For another, medieval Europe *liked* pompous ornament. Knowing this, grouchy monk John Cassian (360–435) drew up a version of the "eight evil thoughts," including vanity and *luxuria*, or reveling in excess. Under the fine leadership of the medieval Church, the eight evil thoughts became the seven deadly sins, which didn't treat vanity as bad enough to be its own sin and limited luxury to lust.

There was still plenty of moralizing about the evils of fancy clothes and excess consumption, because it wouldn't be the medieval Church without some moralizing. During the fifteenth century's very literal bonfires of the vanities, priests urged their audiences to toss their makeup and fancy clothes into the flames, and some people actually did. These clothes weren't merely inappropriate for fighting evil; they *were* evil.

Now, how long their zeal for God-approved austerity lasted is another matter entirely.

Despite their unattractiveness, though, Sicilian statutes from 1290 would seem to suggest the Middle Ages can offer you quite

1   Sarah Grace-Heller, "Angevin-Sicilian Sumptuary Laws of the 1290s: Fashion in the Thirteenth-Century Mediterranean," *Medieval Clothing and Textiles* 11 (2015): 88.

good guidance for figuring out what to wear into actual or metaphorical battle, even if specific types of clothing changed based on time, place, gender, religion, age, class, and occupation. Sometimes it's better to cut things short and move on.

₩ 1. YES, THE MIDDLE AGES OFFER YOU GOOD GUIDANCE

Your Sicilian friends had far more to say about clothing than "don't be a pretentious show-off," and they weren't alone. The 1290 code was one of very, very many so-called sumptuary laws that spread across western Europe from the thirteenth century on. Sumptuary laws could regulate consumption (no, a shared etymology does not count as a bad pun) of any number of goods. But clothing was by far their most common target. Most infamously, sumptuary laws told people what they could and couldn't wear.

This did not mean half of Europe was running around without pants. Statutes were more concerned with who could wear fur, who could wear what kind of fur, who could wear how much fur, who could wear fur in specific places on their outfits and accessories, and mandating that teenage boys in Florence could not wear pink leggings and men in Nuremberg could not wear short jackets. (This last one was the city's prim euphemism for banning a certain practice in which men *enhanced* a certain area of their pants to make it appear larger.)

Sumptuary laws aimed to reinforce social order by restricting various fashions to certain groups, especially by class. For example, people could wear more fur the fur-ther up the social scale they were. (What? You wanted a bad pun.)

Sumptuary laws are practically begging you to go undercover as you begin planning for your quest. Maybe not the ones that differentiated between "the king and everyone else" or "the king on Sundays and the king on every other day." But you could learn which fashions were available to the bourgeoisie or higher, or certain professions of the bourgeoisie or higher, or the nobility or higher. And because most enforcement was left in the hands of people's friends and acquaintances, not actual government officials, there wouldn't be very many people to identify you as someone who shouldn't be wearing *that*.

A Sicilian law that grumbled about "pompous ornaments" in general is even further proof that the Middle Ages can provide great advice for how to dress. This decree was promulgated in the middle of the long-running violent period in the relationship between Aragon and Sicily. So the requirements for men's clothing were understandably centered on what would be more useful in battle—even if it was just to keep the men in a martial mindset. For example, that cloak of yours will be colder and less swanky without a fur lining or even an inner layer of trendy-colored fabric. But it will move much more easily in a fight.

Under this same statute, women, on the other hand, couldn't wear dresses with long trains. In the lawmakers' minds, it had nothing to do with war. No, that fabric wasted on the train could have been donated to poor people.

And all of that business is to say nothing about armor.

The good news for you as a village kid is that chain mail is chain mail. There's only so much that can be done to choose (read: purchase) the "best" metal circles and connectors. I suppose you could be the Emperor Constantine, whose mother placed shards and nails from Jesus's cross inside his *helmet* and turned it into one of the symbols of his imperial status, but heroes shouldn't depend on a literal deus ex machina for protection. So just be sure to pack a fabric surcoat to wear over the top when you're crossing the barren wastes or anywhere else with better weather than England (so . . . everywhere). The sun against shiny metal will not help you stay hydrated.

The better news is that if you're leveling up to plate armor, cities in the fifteenth and sixteenth centuries were in hot competition to make the best armor and get credit for it. (Who needs money when you can build civic pride? Besides everyone?)

Some cities had no hope of catching up to the leaders and didn't even try. Someone has to make the cheap armor, after all—looking at you, London. Nuremberg and Augsburg, though, were fiercely protective of their armor and their armorers. Nuremberg didn't even want the metal its smiths used to make armor to be sold to nonresidents, so the Germans' strategies for keeping it all in the family are pretty much a handbook for picking out the right sword.

You can be somewhat comfortable right away knowing that masters tended to specialize in manufacturing one part of armor, like the Helm-schmieds (translated roughly as "helmet-smiths") of Augsburg being . . . helmet-smiths. If you ask around in a city—or beyond it, even—you can learn the names of the best armorers (like the Helmschmieds). You'll know which master's mark—the proprietary stamp on a piece of armor identify-ing who made it—to look for. Sometimes.

To make sure that the armor was functional, Nuremberg and eventu-ally Augsburg required an inspection of finished armor to make sure every piece of metal contained a sufficient percentage of steel. Unfortunately, they never wrote down how they tested the armor, just that if it didn't pass, it should be smashed. Hopefully not while you're wearing it.

While "torn apart" served as a good way to identify armor that didn't pass the tests, inspectors preferred to add a mark of their own to signify what was good quality. For Nuremberg, it was the city's symbol of a proud eagle. In 1461, Augsburg's guild suggested its armorers stamp on their city's symbol: a pine cone. Yes, really. In medieval Christianity, pine cones symbolized resurrection, which is probably the one thing more useful in battle than armor.

❦ 2. No, the Middle Ages Do Not Offer You Good Guidance

Sumptuary laws can teach you how to *dress* to fight evil; armoring codes teach you how to dress to *fight* evil . . .

A brief word about using laws as historical sources.

Laws are an excellent guide to a society's ideals, or at least a compro-mise thereabout. They're a bit troublesome for figuring out what people were really doing. A statute might ban a practice because the lawmakers were worried that someone might do it even though no one was, or because everyone was doing it, or anything in between. More relevant for your purposes is the knowledge that the existence of a law does not mean it was followed.

For example, you can probably guess how strict people were about following sumptuary laws and armoring statutes.

Some Italian cities couldn't even find people willing to enforce their sumptuary laws. Official positions overseeing their enforcement stayed vacant. Subsequent laws upped the bounty that residents received for turning in their rule-breaking neighbors. Then there were the "letter of the law but not the spirit" people, whose strategies included sneakily dying a common type of fur to look like a more prestigious kind.

At least their charade suggests how you can disguise yourself for less money.

It would be nice if armor codes did better in practice, but even here there's a bit of hope involved. The presence of Nuremberg's mark for quality metal in armor doesn't relate very strongly to the composition of surviving armor, even though the city was quite shrill about people imitating its mark to pass off lousy armor as prestigious Nuremberg material. (Don't be like Fritz Paursmid, who spent four weeks of 1502 in jail for using a master's mark deemed too close to Nuremberg's eagle.)

In the end, then, medieval sources do offer some guidance on figuring out how to dress for fighting evil in whatever time and place you find yourself. But sumptuary laws and armoring codes provide guidelines, not certainties. So be grateful that you have a base to work from and that you don't have to adhere to these laws obsessively. You've got evil to fight—you don't have time to let pink leggings and ermine lining, shall we say, *consume* you.

Okay, sometimes a shared etymology is no excuse.

23

At the Inn

HOW *to* FIND *the* INN

I n fourteenth-century London, the smallest amount of ale you could generally buy was a quart. Not a cup, not a pint—a quart. Further, innkeepers were legally required to lock the doors of their inns at night: no one in, no one out. These policies were not at all related.

On your quest through the medieval world, you'll need to sleep at some point, and you'll probably want to be under something besides the stars. You might not have to stay at an inn, however. The early medieval Islamic world developed a network of combination inn/trading depots for merchants called funduqs. They had a less unsavory reputation than inns in the west. And all you'd have to do to qualify as a guest would be to possess the tangible trade goods that you can't exactly carry if you're fleeing a supernatural army.

For a good alternative, get religion! Churches and monasteries were required by the Church to offer overnight sanctuary to all comers (which all too often meant nobles and however much of their traveling party would fit), and religious principles of hospitality were just as deeply rooted in Judaism and Islam.

The list of possibilities of where to stay could unroll almost forever, ending with the one even your little village knew and feared—namely, the legal obligation to give quarter to any passing pilgrims or stationed soldiers. No matter how long a family had to sleep in an attic or shed.

But let's face it: You have no problem with the crying babies you'd probably have to deal with if you demanded shelter in a private home. But you know all about quartering troops firsthand, and you don't want to make another family nervous about an overnight stranger. The insides of churches or mosques or synagogues? Been there, done that. It's the late Middle Ages in western Europe, and you want a nice quart of ale and a bar fight. You're heading for an inn.

✹ HOW YOU'LL FIND THE INN

Inns represented opportunities to make money (whether making money involved charging for rooms or something less legal), as they were places that saw a lot of travelers. In general, they'd be located in places with a lot of traffic—in towns, at pilgrimage sites, along major routes. Even better for you, they could also be found in suburbs (yes, suburbs) or on the outskirts of towns, where you wouldn't have to pay city tolls to enter.

If you end up in a town (which you will; heroes do), you're going to have a bit of a challenge. In 1309, London had 354 tax-paying taverns. The ones that didn't accept overnight guests were probably balanced out by the number of one-night pop-ups just unofficial enough to escape taxes. In other words, there probably won't be an "inn quarter" or "Tavern Street."

As you wind through the complex of streets, you'll be scanning buildings for the graphic signs that single out inns. In almost any city, innkeepers would hang wreaths from poles, but there were plenty of local variations that a traveler would have to ask about. (For example, in Paris, plenty of signs featured images of saints. Can't fault people for wishful thinking.)

But with 354 taverns in London, there were 354 taverns competing for business. Innkeepers needed to make their establishments stand out. They usually settled on the incredibly novel strategy of coming up with names. That's not to say they were creative names: When William Porland recorded the names of fifty taverns in the fifteenth century, six of them were called the Swan. But it wasn't really the innkeepers' fault. There was no reason to distinguish an inn by a written-out name when literacy rates maxed out in the 30 to 40 percent range, which meant a 60 to 70 percent chance that the clientele couldn't read a name and the innkeepers them-

27

selves couldn't write it. Businesses often took on the names of sign-friendly graphic symbols that would be quick to catch the eye. This often led to inns adopting heraldic symbols, because everyone would recognize their meaning. The same emblems that knights and noble families adopted to signify the pride and prestige of their lineage were identifiers of places where you could watch other people get drunk and do stupid things.

Not *every* inn used a heraldic charge as its sign and name. Saints' iconography was popular, of course, meaning that you could drink at a good assortment of Katherine Wheels—you know, the gruesome device built specifically to torture St. Katherine of Alexandria.

In other words, pay some attention after you walk into the inn, too.

❦ WHAT YOU'LL FIND AT THE INN

An inn that you stumble upon in the west (outside of the Islamic regions of Iberia) isn't going to be one of those three-hundred-bed funduqs in Cairo or anything nice like that. But by the late 1300s, any respectable city is going to have at least one respectable inn with up to twenty small guest chambers, or fewer but larger dorms.

You, of course, will not be able to afford this.

Not that you'll be able to tell by looking whether an inn is sufficiently disreputable to fit your budget. In towns, at least, inns tended to blend right in with the other buildings in the cityscape, maybe even being indistinguishable from the ordinary houses or shop-and-apartment buildings on either side. And why not, since inns were often based on household layout and even run as family businesses?

Whether you enter directly off the street or climb up to a second floor above a space for stabling guests' horses, you'll step into a common room containing one or more tables, benches, and inn guests eager to teach you new definitions of ignominious. The kitchen and maybe the latrine will attach directly to the common rooms, but hopefully not to each other.

As with apartments above regular businesses, you'll make a deal with the innkeeper for a bed (well, part of a bed) in the sleeping quarters upstairs.

Ideally, you'll reach your (very shared) room by stairs. The alternative was by ladder, an interesting design choice considering the common room was essentially a bar.

♛ WHO YOU'LL FIND

Sorry to kill your romantic dreams of going somewhere solo—no quest succeeds without a full traveling party, and a tavern common room offers your most fertile recruiting ground. After all, every innkeeper seeks to make their guests spend as much time as possible in full view, which is to say, spend as much money as possible on drinks and food. Taverns catering to a local clientele were sometimes patronized by men (and the occasional woman) practicing the same craft or other job. But on the road, all bets were off except the ones placed over dice and chess.

You'll see pilgrims, messengers, petty merchants, servants, soldiers, new immigrants—anyone whose money a particular innkeeper was willing to accept. There would still be more men than women; Greek miracle stories and Italian farces show that rape was a very real threat for women staying in inns, and gaining a bad reputation was almost inevitable. It won't surprise you to see people with all sorts of skin colors, especially the closer you get to the Mediterranean.

Taverns and inns had a staff too—possibly just the members of the family who owned it and a couple of servants. And then there were the nonstaff "workers" there to earn whatever money they could. Like the bard in the corner.

Did I mention there would be a bard?

HOW *to* PUT UP *with the* BARD

ut up with"? Why the pessimism?

It's the Middle Ages! The age of romance, of poetry, of song! An age of music like none other! Don't believe me? Then let's take a look at ninth-century Samarra, near Baghdad, where rival celebrity divas cultivated fan bases who reportedly *hated* one another. In fifteenth-century England, the official band of York went on tour to play concerts in other cities. Twelfth-century France saw accusations of behind-the-scenes sex and other debauchery. And, of course, Palestine at the turn of the fifth century had a scholar who spent much of his life living in a cave, ranting about popular music as a gateway to worshipping demons.

Truly, an age like *none* other.

The chance to explore entire worlds through music will be one of the most exciting (and least deadly, for that matter) things about your quest. According to romance poet Jean Renart, at the beginning of the thirteenth century, singers performed alone or were accompanied by a type of fiddle called a vielle. You might hear trumpets, flutes, pipes, other wind or string instruments, or drums that could drown out the thunder. Or you could get really lucky with two for the price of one: the very popular pipe and tabour consisted of a flute and drum played at the same time, by the same person.

To hear all these melodies, you didn't have to be in cities or courts. Like the York town musicians, plenty of Europe's best instrumentalists and singers put in their fair share of travel. In 1372, for example, Prince Juan I of Aragon paid to send four of his court musicians to

Flanders, where they could get up to speed on the hottest music trends. On the way home, they were directed to stop in Paris and play for the French king. Relevant detail: Juan trusted that his musicians were good enough for the other king to see their performance as a gift, instead of bad enough for the other king to start a war.

Not everyone could afford to be so trusting. Medieval Europe had its great musicians, and then its musicians who dreamed of being great. Especially at inns and on the road.

There was another way that medieval musical culture was truly like no other that ever existed: its high number of musicians with no other appreciable skills. When minstrel guilds like that in York got their cities to ban performances by nonmembers, and guilds' primary responsibility was quality control . . .

Oh. That's why the pessimism.

So yes, when the pesky and overly enthusiastic bard won't let you stop them from joining your traveling party, you're going to need some strategies to deal with it.

♜ STRATEGY #1: BE DEAF

The medieval world was not generally kind to people with disabilities—it's pretty telling that much of the evidence about their lives comes from stories of their miraculous "cures." But that hardly means deaf people were helpless. One village in 1270s Switzerland invented a rudimentary sign language for a deaf-mute boy named Louis, who made himself into a successful blacksmith.

So why not turn *your* disability into an advantage when you can? Deaf Spanish nun Teresa de Cartagena (her surname, not birthplace) sure did. In medieval western Europe, the primary responsibility of nuns and monks was to *sing* prayers every day, for most of the day (and night). Teresa (born around 1420) used her deafness as an inspiration to write two books. In the first, *Grove of the Infirm*, she turned the social downsides of deafness—such as the inability to hear religious music and fully participate in prayers—into internal fruits that shut out the world to help deaf people focus on God. In her second book, *Wonder at the Works of God,* she politely gave people who insulted her a very, very long list of reasons they were wrong.

Oh, and Teresa is one of Spain's earliest known women writers.

Be like Teresa. Rejoice in your ability to tune out that bard without even trying, and tease the people who can't.

✷ STRATEGY #2: BIDE YOUR TIME

If you can only imitate Teresa's subtle revenge on those who bullied her, just grit your teeth and wait for your bard to slip up like traveling entertainer "Monsieur Cruche" did in 1515 Paris. He wrote and apparently performed something described as simultaneously a sermon and a farce, which got him hauled before King Francis I. That the central characters of this farce were very unsubtly Francis and his mistress might have had something to do with that.

As the rumor went, at least, Francis decreed that Cruche should be stripped to his underwear and whipped. Granted, those screams might not be quite enough music to your ears to make up for all the pain the bard has caused your eardrums, but it's a start. Francis certainly thought it wasn't enough, because he also wanted Cruche to be tied inside a sack and thrown right out the window into the river below.

However, it seems that Cruche got out of the finale of his punishment by claiming he was a priest and only subject to ecclesiastical law, etc., etc. Apparently Francis forgot that Cruche was an *actor,* and the members of his court were secretly delighted enough by the farce to stay quiet.

And no, in your case, there's no chance you'll be lucky enough that the bard will repent their ways and find a new career. But don't despair! Cruche's escape highlights three very relevant points for you as you journey. First, having a member of your party who's skilled at disguising themselves as a person with strong social standing *will* be helpful. Second, the standard way to claim benefit of clergy in the late Middle Ages was to show you could read Latin, a skill that will also prove useful. Third, the rumors that popularized Cruche's story likely repeated the farce's contents correctly and almost certainly exaggerated the potential punishment. So even if your entire party gets blamed for your bard being . . . a bard, you probably won't die.

❦ STRATEGY #3: GET RICH

If you can't be like Teresa and focus on God, be yourself and focus on greed.

Musical performance in the Middle Ages could be a surprisingly lucrative profession. Some instrumentalists and singers were full-time, salaried employees of city governments. Rigord (c. 1148–c. 1208), a French royal historian, noted that kings paid their entertainers in gold, silver, horses, and robes worth enough money to feed someone for a year. In Iraq and al-Andalus, enslaved women composers and singers were known to become wealthy enough to buy themselves out of slavery. Yes, even if your eardrums hurt while you travel with the bard, you will be able to remind yourself that it's far nicer to be able to afford an inn than to sleep in a tent.

"Will" is such a subjective word, isn't it?

Late medieval cities were filled with individual opportunities for musicians to perform for a fee—playing for social dances or in-home private shows, accompanying processions, providing the soundtrack to the calendar of annual religious dramas. Some minstrels were able to befriend a tavern keeper or two, and got them to charge admission on scheduled performance nights. You just don't want your bard to be barber-surgeon, singer, and poet Hans Folz (c. 1435–1513). The city of Nuremberg passed a law banning him—specifically him, by name—from charging admission to tavern performances of his works.

But cities were also filled with professional musicians wanting to get paid for what they did, and amateur musicians from the bourgeoisie and upper class with the connections to get those roles. (That would include Folz, who was apparently rich enough to buy or rent a printing press.) Other musicians—and even the lucky ones between their paying gigs— had to depend on enough people tossing a coin or two to them. And what

33

part of your quest so far has made you think the bard insisting on coming along is even good enough to play at dances?

Strategy #3 seems less than strategic.

✿ REPLACEMENT FOR STRATEGY #3: CUDDLE WITH THEIR PETS

Most musical performances in the Middle Ages blended into other types of entertainment, like reciting King Arthur stories or acting the fool. Like everyone's favorite undefenestrated entertainer Monsieur Cruche, itinerant bards often developed other skills that gave them flexibility in employment but still left them sleeping in tents.

If you can't be like Teresa, if the bard never gets what's coming, or if they leave you with even less money than you had when you started, well, then you can find your consolation in the most popular second profession: animal trainer.

Nobles from Burgundy to the Swahili city-states to Baghdad to India to China were well-known for keeping menageries for display or performance of tricks. Their collections were typically composed of exotic animals like lions and elephants. And as they needed their animals to perform tricks, they had to bring their pets along on the journey. People in the Middle Ages understood full well the importance of human closeness for training animals, too. One English hunting manual even recommended having someone sleep in future hunting dogs' kennels to keep the puppies company. (Best. job. *ever*.) If your eardrums throb during the day, you can at least take consolation in cuddling with furry cuteness at night.

Oh. Right. Itinerant animal trainers in England were known as bear-wards. Because the animals they trained were bears. About that "cuddling" . . .

✿ REPLACEMENT FOR THE REPLACEMENT FOR STRATEGY #3: LEARN TO SING

Be the bard. Make everyone else put up with *you*.

HOW *to* BEAT *the* CHEATS

enry Pecche had survived the Black Death. But would he survive lunch?

On the mean streets of medieval London, it was hardly a given. Cooks were infamous for stuffing ashes, sand, and "coppewebbes" into their breads and pies to puff up their size and weight.[2] And on that fateful day in January 1351, Pecche and two of his friends made the mistake of stopping for chicken turnovers at the stand run by Henry de Passelewe. Chicken turnovers that were, in the words of the jury, "putrid and stinking, and an abomination to mankind."[3]

Chicken turnovers that Pecche and his friends had devoured most of before they found this out.

So come lunchtime, don't be like Pecche. Don't spend the money or the hours vomiting up three-quarters of a rotten chicken, buying beer at illegal prices, or consuming bread loaves made of horse feed. All too many vendors were eager to skim that last penny, including charging you extra to pay with pennies instead of coins of larger denominations so they could "modify" the exchange rate.

You, of course, would never be so devious. So, you'll just have to learn about scams to avoid, at the inn and beyond, from things like law codes and merchants' handbooks. (What to *avoid*, you understand.) As you might expect, the menu of cons starts with alcohol.

---

2   Henry Thomas Riley (ed.), *Munimenta Gildhallae Londoniensis* (Longman, Green, Longman, and Roberts, 1860), 3: 415.
3   Henry Thomas Riley (ed. and trans.), *Memorials of London and London Life in the XIIIth, XIVth, and XVth Centuries: Being a Series of Extracts, Local, Social, and Political, from the Early Archives of the City of London* (Longmans, 1868), 266.

Alcohol's prominence on the list of scams was even more nefarious than it might seem at first. Plenty of water was available to drink, as long as it was "sweet water" instead of "bitter water," or perhaps bitter water that had been boiled. But wine, beer, and ale were the all day, every day drinks for Christians and Jews of all ages—the helpful extra calories and taste more or less made them the medieval version of soda.

Still, the number of preachers yelling about how drinking to get drunk was an especially egregious sin suggests that the drinks you're going to order at the tavern create some additional factors to consider before you imbibe.

The oldest scheme is ancient—as in biblical. Sell the good wine with meals, but as the evening wears on, slip in cheaper and cheaper types to people who can no longer tell the difference. The innkeeper might also lie about which is the good wine and where it's from in the first place. For example, Augsburg vendors could sell all the French wine they wanted. They were merely banned from selling German wine while claiming it was from France.

You can't get scammed over an evening of drinks if you don't have the money in the first place. No, if someone needed to fund a frantic escape or a quest, you—I mean, they—should wheedle their way into the spice trade. Given the loose western European definition of spice as "something expensive from far away," you can be confident that with a few good days of work, you'll either be really rich or really in jail.

As with all true international traders, bribes are just another line to itemize in your budget. You've got *real* scams to run—I mean, to worry about. Spices were sold by weight in large, bundled quantities, and generally on the basis of small samples. So, don't let the seller choose the sample for you. You can't trust anyone.

In the course of your quest, you should expect to face sellers who tare their scales unfairly. Or, as an example that takes things one step further, the Venetians grumped about Armenian wheat traders, who (according to the Venetians) invented their own weight measures altogether. You're a foreigner; what do you know? And even balancing out a scale to both sides' satisfaction won't prevent a vendor from giving the weight of their product a little boost.

Honestly (. . .), you should be expecting a certain amount of sand or dust mixed into any spice you buy. Really—London had an actual guild of people whose job it was to sort out the actual spices. Of course, if you were the one selling it *to* a London merchant, the so-called garblers wouldn't help; and if you were the London merchant *buying* the spice, you'd pay the garblers instead; indeed, it was a business in which everyone was as dirty as their sacks.

And before you go thinking that sand is the only problem you'll face, the fourteenth-century book *Zibaldone da Canal*—you want to use the Italian title because it's more fun to say than "scrapbook of someone probably from the da Canal family"—includes a massive section explaining how to identify a quality spice from a knockoff.

With spices, as with almost any food-related product you may want to buy, the best way to detect a problem is to taste the sample. Mind you, two of the more valuable spices were tutty and ambergris, which is to say chimney scrapings and dried whale vomit—so not everything is going to taste *good*. And from that end, not everything is meant to be tasted at all. Orpiment was a mineral used in dyes. It was fine if fresh, but degraded, it became . . . arsenic.

In the end, the spice trade as a whole functioned because traders depended on reputation and repeat business. Unlike an innkeeper who could reel in one-time foreign visitors, merchants would be out of business if they became known for conning people more often than other merchants did. Unless, of course, a merchant similarly specialized in one-off transactions.

So, my dear first-time foreign visitor, be careful what you eat.

HOW *to* FLIRT *with the* BARMAID

ey, baby, want to go back to my monastery and discuss our celibacy vows?

Hold up there, tiger or tigress. (Point of order: medieval descriptions of tigers describe cheetahs.) Chivalry is for nobles, especially for noblemen who want to pretend they're knights glowing with battle glory. For you, on the other hand, there are two possible outcomes for flirting with the barmaid during a quest. First, she pretends to play hard to get and finds an excuse to join your party. Second, someone sees you flirting and gets angry, and after the ensuing bar fight, she's forced to flee along with the rest of your party.

So don't worry that your best pickup line is *I'm afraid I'll have to hang you from my gallows, because you just stole my heart.* You've got three other questions to consider before you're remotely ready to speak aloud. Can you flirt with a barmaid? Do you want to flirt with a barmaid? And finally, should you flirt with a barmaid?

❧ CAN YOU FLIRT WITH A BARMAID?

Nothing is fair in love or war, so this question itself has three subquestions.

Can You Flirt With a Barmaid?

Hey, baby, want to go confess the sin of lust?

Your pickup line is just like a city in Europe: hearing it will kill people faster than new ones can be born to replace them. When medieval European towns were called "population sinks," it wasn't because people went there to get clean. Because no matter how much you may want to, you can't flirt with a barmaid if she's died of plague.

But while natives alone couldn't make their cities grow and prosper, immigrants got the job done. Over the course of the Middle Ages, urban populations exploded as people moved from the countryside to nearby cities in search of work. The closer you went to Belgium, the more teenage and twentysomething women hoping to earn their way to bigger dowries you would see. (Belgium, that famous land of love.)

In other words: you can indeed flirt with a barmaid, because a whole lot of young urban women are single, working, and looking for a long-term relationship.

But . . .

Can You *Flirt* With a Barmaid?

You might have to burn at the stake, baby, because you just cast a spell on me.

Your pickup lines are like a medieval marriage: not so good when arranged in advance.

It was a borderline requirement for marriages among Europe's upper crust to be arranged, and for every other reason in the world than mutual attraction. If you're so bad at flirting that *Hey, baby, wanna come to a joust? I can show you the difference between a knight and a squire* is the best you can do, then a means of courtship that precludes flirting should come as a relief.

But if you meet the legal requirements for marrying the barmaid (male and at least fourteen years old; she only has to be twelve), hold on. You probably want to talk to Jeanne d'Albret of Navarre and William, duke of a lot less territory than he wanted.

Jeanne's parents (that would be the king and queen of Navarre) had arranged a marriage between their daughter and William, a German duke with delusions of rebelling against the Holy Roman emperor. On her wedding day in 1541, the *twelve-year-old* princess had to be carried down the

39

aisle of the church—sobbing. Subsequently, William's rebellion ended poorly, as did his marriage, with Jeanne winning an annulment in 1545.

On the other hand, Jeanne participated eagerly in the arrangement of her marriage with Antoine de Bourbon in 1548, a marriage that would eventually make her son the king of Navarre—and the king of *France*. When she fell out of love with her husband, she said, "No matter," and concentrated on aiding the rise of his house. She made herself the leader of the heretical Protestant movement in France and Navarre, and then declared it the official religion of Navarre. The little girl who sobbed at her first marriage became the leader who *made Catholicism a heresy* during her second.

Arranged marriages: just don't do it. Which brings us to:

Can You Flirt With a Barmaid?

We've established this.

No.

❧ Do You Want to Flirt With a Barmaid?

Did I just walk into the Renaissance? Because you are truly a work of art.

Your pickup lines are just like 10 to 25 percent of women in medieval cities: never going to end up in marriage.

That number doesn't mean 10 to 25 percent of medieval women, not counting nuns, were exclusively attracted to other women. (And it definitely doesn't mean that 10 to 25 percent of them are attracted to *you*.) Male writers spent enough time defining women by sex; don't help them! Medieval women could stay single for the independence, or because they didn't want kids, or out of religious desire, or for a thousand other reasons that we'll never know because women didn't write them down.

On the other hand, the lives of those (legally) single women offer glimpses into ways that medieval women who loved women—be it crush or girl crush—might have arranged their lives together. In 1493, Thomasina of (presumably) London shared a room in London with a woman identified only as "a concubine." Gertrude of Offenburg (d. 1335) was a wealthy widow who opened her house to Heilke of Staufenburg, a young unmarried woman. The two of them schemed to win Heilke's full inheritance from her brothers to better support themselves, and stayed together until Gertrude's death—thirty years and twenty-eight weeks later. Nicole of Rubercy and a woman identified only as Contesse rented rooms in the same hostel around 1270. Despite their own poverty, they each worked extra jobs when the other was sick in order to support them both.

Again, don't draw conclusions about any particular case here. They provide templates for same-sex love. Undoubtedly, though, they show that medieval Europe had *perfected* the art of the girl crush. As was said about Gertrude and Heilke, "Together, they shared a household and suffered together through both bad and good just as if it were meant for both of them. When one of them was ailing, so was the other . . . They helped each other to bear this suffering as friends in the name of God. And they lived a happy and blessed life together."[4]

So if you think she's cute, why not flirt with the barmaid? It may or may not be 10 to 25 percent exactly, but there's a good chance she'll flirt back.

Which brings us to the final question. Male, female; married, single; attracted to her or not . . .

❦ SHOULD YOU FLIRT WITH THE BARMAID?

Hey, baby, wanna come to my castle and explore a tower?

Your pickup lines are like bar fights: they have no place in a family establishment. And guess what: there's a high chance the alehouse you're patronizing is indeed a family establishment.

Maybe a father owned the tavern on the bottom floor of his house and trained his son to take over the family business. A mother set up some

---

4   Anneke Mulder-Bakker, *The Dedicated Spiritual Life of Upper Rhine Noblewomen: A Study and Translation of a Fourteenth-Century Spiritual Biography of Gertrude Rickeldey of Ortenberg and Heilke of Staufenberg* (Brepols, 2017), 131.

tables from time to time, when her husband's income had taken a dip. A widow converted part of her house into a public space.

Yes, sometimes a medieval tavern was a classic stand-alone business, with a stand-alone building, maybe its own brewery, and a large staff who served in various roles. (And yes, sometimes "tavern" was a euphemism.) But even into the early modern era, which saw a general reduction in formal employment options open to women, smaller taverns were common, often woman-owned businesses that were operated out of a home and run by a family—the *whole* family.

Jacques le Francois was reminded of this arrangement one year in Pitres as he was minding his own business over a quiet mug of ale—and for no reason at all, the tavern keeper's family tried to throw him out of the house. (The tavern owner's account of the incident, unsurprisingly, filled in the blanks behind "no reason at all" with Jacques being a violent, drunken lout who attacked the family. A neighbor's account of the incident filled in the blank behind "being a violent, drunken lout" with "Jacques and the tavern keeper's family were feuding over some land.")

In other words, that barmaid stands a good chance of being the tavern keeper's daughter. And even if she's a servant, well, medieval men and women sued their servants *frequently* for courting and marrying without their permission.

The innkeepers are on their guard for stopping patrons' violence, for getting customers drunk enough to buy more ale or beer, and for watering down ale or beer to make a larger profit. But if they're even slightly good parents or employers, and "tavern" is not a euphemism, they're probably also keeping half an eye on that cute barmaid—and on *you*.

Whether you're male, female, nonbinary, or an amoeba that reproduces by splitting in half, sometimes flirting with the barmaid is just a plain old bad idea. If good ol' Jacques is any indication, that family will do what it must to protect its own.

So, about that bar fight.

HOW *to* WIN *the* BAR FIGHT

erball was drunk. Drunk, drunk, *drunk*. This was a problem because it was 860, and he was king of Osraige, and the Vikings were attacking. As in, attacking his home. As in, right now. As in, they were right outside. And as his nobles informed him, "Drunkenness is the enemy of valor."

But Cerball seized his sword anyway. As the Old Irish chronicle puts it: "This is how Cerball came out of his chamber: with a huge royal candle before him, and the light of that candle shone far in every direction. Great terror seized the Norwegians, and they fled to the nearby mountains and to the woods. Those who stayed behind out of valor, moreover, were all killed."[5]

Oh, that's not what you meant by "bar fight"?

No matter. Medieval court records can fill up any rogue's book of tricks.

❦ 1. LONDON, NOVEMBER 1321

Michael le Gaugeour ("le" was common in medieval English surnames) and John Faukes were playing a dice game called "hasard"— supposedly invented by worn-out Crusaders between battles—in an Abbechirchelane inn. *Something* happened, for sure, because John didn't go home. He lay in wait outside the tavern. And when Michael emerged, John stabbed him in the heart with a sword. The coroner reported that the wound was nearly six inches deep.

---

5   Joan N. Radner (trans.), *Fragmentary Annals of Ireland* (University College Cork CELT Project, 2004, 2008), https://celt.ucc.ie/published/T100017.html, FA 277.

John found temporary sanctuary with some monks, and then vanished from the city altogether. So that's a pretty good way to win a bar fight.

❧ 2. LONDON, DECEMBER 1323

Stephen de Lenne ("de" was also common in medieval English surnames) and Arcus de Rikelinge had placed bets on the outcome of their game of backgammon, and Stephen won handily. The two men left the inn together, walking and chatting. Until Arcus drew a knife and stabbed Stephen in the stomach. Twice. Including a four-inch wound.

Arcus escaped.

❧ 3. MEUNG-SUR-LOIRE, 1341

Agnes la Paganam (actually French for once) had sworn the field was Guerin le Pioner's to harvest. But she had gathered a group and gotten there first. And all Guerin did was storm into her tavern, call her a lying whore, and threaten to burn it down.

Oh, until he sued her, and won, and she had to cough up 100 livres. Winning a bar fight in your opponent's own bar is some next-level skill.

❧ 4. LONDON, MARCH 1301

Robert de Exeter, Roger de Lincoln, Henry de Lincoln, and the barmaid Leticia were very much *not* playing checkers. But Thomas de Bristoll and Joice de Cornwall were. And either Robert, Roger, or Henry decided the checkerboard looked like the perfect place for sex. One of the men sprawled on the bench with Leticia, scattering the checker pieces everywhere.

Subsequent events are rather murky, but somehow it was Thomas who ended up stripped down to his underwear and hiding upstairs. Robert ended up with Thomas's hidden dagger, while Joice ended up dead in the street.

Robert, Roger, and Henry escaped, and Thomas learned a valuable lesson about carrying a concealed weapon.

✤ 5. WESTMINSTER, 1397

Visiting priest Simon Helgey probably had more on his mind than thirst when he stepped into the Cock Inn. Owner Alice atte Hethe also had more on her mind. As soon as she lured Helgey into her inn, her friends pounced on him. Simon was left ring-less, purse-less, coat-less, and penniless.

Simon probably learned to try harder at his celibacy vow.

✤ 6. OXFORD, 1306

Elyas of Wales and two other men tried to vandalize a private inn and rape its owner, Margery de la Marche. She screamed for help so loudly that it could be heard in the street and inside nearby houses. The two friends fled into the street, but neighbor John cornered Elyas in the basement. Elyas tried to fight his way free, breaking John's forearm, but John just kept blocking the stairs—and punching him in the face.

While everyone lost in that bar fight, Margery and John had the last laugh. The local jailer was John's father.

✤ 7. MUNICH, 1513

One moment, Jorg Rigler and an unnamed servant of famous knight Caspar Wintzer were sharing a cup of wine. The next moment, they were making a pact to leave the tavern and murder the first person they met.

As the sun faded from the sky, that first unfortunate man begged for his life. He'd done nothing wrong—he wasn't a threat—look, he'd lost a hand in a previous accident and *couldn't* be a threat! So Rigler and the servant killed the second man they saw instead. The servant was arrested, blamed Rigler, and was executed. Rigler may have been arrested, definitely blamed the servant, and definitely escaped.

But you can rarely escape divine justice. Two years later, Rigler was drunk, fell down some stairs, and died.

And then there's one final trick, deployed only by the bravest of souls in the most fearsome of circumstances. Like, say, the morning after Cerball fended off the Vikings with a candle and his sword. Because at dawn, the surviving Vikings came back. Cerball led the charge against them. And as the chronicle says: "Cerball himself fought hard in this battle, and the amount he had drunk the night before hampered him greatly, and he vomited much, and that gave him immense strength."[6] He returned home laden with glory and spoils.

Scratch all of the above. *That* is how you win a bar fight.

6 *Fragmentary Annals*, FA 277.

HOW *to* ESCAPE *the* INN

n twelfth-century Genoa, the leading families built tall, graceful towers next to their homes. The towers illustrated the city's power and wealth, its dominance of so much of the lucrative trans-Mediterranean trade.

Then the families built catapults on top of the towers, so they could fling large rocks at the other towers and knock them down.

It was the endgame of a centuries-old war among shifting family alliances that had included, among other things, a murder in the middle of a city council meeting. In the Middle Ages, memories were long and feuds did *not* mess around.

Which is to say: so, about that bar fight.

❧ ESCAPING THE CITY: WHO

Yes, people are going to find out about your bar fight. And no, their discovery is not going to go well for you. Win or lose (and with instructions like mine, how could you lose?), you'll be the one escaping the city.

In later medieval Europe, "word on the street" had a formal Latin name (*fama*), so you can already tell it's a big deal. Far more than just potential evidence in court or a bad time in grammar school, *fama* could be both judge and jury.

The core of *fama* was having a "good name" or a "bad name." Which is to say, the legal consequences of your fight could depend on who had an established good reputation—which is a preestablished bad thing for you as an out-of-towner.

One French law textbook offered a sample case directly relevant to your present circumstance. The theoretical victim is staying at an inn, and their belongings vanish. If the innkeeper has a bad reputation, it was almost a foregone conclusion that they had stolen the guest's property. But if the innkeeper had good *fama* . . . had there even been a crime in the first place?

This case was just theoretical, and things may not have been so extreme in reality. But who are you to be so lucky?

❧ ESCAPING THE CITY: WHY

Nothing says "tavern" like violence. In fact, if you found a room in one of those inns whose regulars were bandits plotting a robbery, they might be more suspicious of a lack of bar fighting. (On the other hand, if you're in that tavern, you probably fought one of those bandits. You definitely don't want to stick around.)

Those court cases, though, show that medieval Europeans were mostly (*mostly*) opposed to violence even in its most expected environments. The Genoans only flung rocks at other towers *sometimes*. This dedication to mostly preventing violence played out in both law and practice. In some places, neighbors and bystanders who didn't throw themselves into stopping a fight or chasing down a bad guy could be charged with a crime themselves.

Just as relevant for you, people sometimes went to impressive lengths to prevent violence before it began, even at risk to their own lives. In 1565 Frankfurt am Main, resolutely middle-class Hans Heckpecher rode his donkey through a narrow gate into the city at the exact moment one of the city's wealthy residents wished to leave. Philipp Weiss von Limburg suddenly decided he wasn't in so much of a rush after all. He yanked the other man off his donkey and brandished a knife.

48 The sources aren't clear whether the city guards maintained their stony watch over the town gate or rubbernecked the fight. The point is

that they didn't get involved. The random Frankfurters in that street, however, did. One of them stepped between Heckpecher and Weiss with his own knife, yelling at them to calm down. You can imagine the extent of his success.

But he wasn't alone—other bystanders jumped in to try to hold Heckpecher and Weiss back from jumping at each other. In fact, after a brief burst of surprised curse words when Weiss first pulled him off his donkey, even Heckpecher (supposedly) tried to approach Weiss unarmed with an appeal to keep the peace. Even with guards right there, ordinary townspeople played major roles in the situation, ending with neither party dead. Weiss tried to stab one of them, and still they kept trying.

So even if your onlookers *expected* a bar fight, they probably didn't *want* a bar fight.

Suddenly this inn and this city aren't looking so welcoming after all.

❧ ESCAPING THE CITY: WHEN

Don't be daft.

Now.

❧ ESCAPING THE CITY: HOW

You'll have an easier time if it's daylight (which it's likely not). First, you have to get ahead of the gossip. News of a crime and a criminal could technically travel at the speed of horse. In practice, medieval cities had "speed limits" consisting of "not almost trampling small children" and enforced by other townspeople. So for the most part, *fama* traveled at the speed of human feet or comprehensible yelling. And lest you think of hiding out until people forget, consider that medieval Parisians, at least, were known to track down criminals well after the fact.

To avoid provoking general suspicion, you'll need to either blend in or stand out in the right way. The first option was mostly a matter of wearing clothing with the appropriate local touches. The riskier option was to dress up in a different city's twist on current upscale clothing—and it was vital

49

to pick the right city. By 1500, quite a few towns had agreements with each other that merchants from one were covered by their home laws even in the other city (as long as there was no murder or arson involved, which in your case, *hmm*).

Since the sun has already set at a time appropriate to your latitude, you've got some additional problems.

The first is straight-up getting to where you're going. Even if you magically know the city's layout, there's the minor glitch of not being able to *see* whether you're going in the right direction. The multistory buildings lining narrow streets may well overshadow any moonlight. Cities at constant risk of enemy infiltration or attack, like in the Iberian interior, often passed laws declaring that only city watchmen could carry torches at night.

Your easiest solution is to pretend to be a town guard. Since guard duty was often assigned as a temporary rotation with new faces all the time, impersonating a guard was surprisingly plausible.

Unfortunately, this solution was also all too plausible to the city's militia leaders. They developed—I'm not kidding—a rotation of code words that guards would recite to each other as they passed in the streets during their rounds, or if someone had reason to leave through the gate.

If absolutely all else fails for you, your final, scorched-earth option is to start a fire as a distraction. There was almost no greater danger to a medieval city than fire, and no faster way to draw the attention and involvement of anyone nearby.

But put this tactic out of your mind. Setting a fire as a weapon against the city makes you guilty of arson and treason immediately, not to mention murder for any deaths that might result. Which means that you're looking at *two* death-penalty crimes right from the start. And law codes tended to dictate specific types of execution for the various capital crimes. Most important, you're a hero. Heroes are *accused* of arson and murder. They don't actually *commit* them.

But if all else fails, you can still break into one of those Italian family towers, load up the catapult, and get to work. If flinging rocks from a tower to smash apart your rivals' palaces won't be enough of a distraction to help you escape and get you back on the road, nothing will.

ON the ROAD

ON *the* (LITERAL) ROAD

hen you're being chased down the road by the angry mother of that barmaid and eventually also an army of evil made manifest, you'd better hope you're nowhere near the abbey of Chertsey in the 1380s. If a traveler needed one last overnight stop on the road to London, sure, the monks would welcome them gladly. But their hospitality definitely came with a caveat. For instance, there was that one road away from the monastery that they hadn't built yet. On the road they *did* build, there was that one part by the river where, when the river flooded, it overflowed its banks and turned the road into a lake. There was also that other part of the road where the abbey had sunk a well in the middle. And that *other* part of the road where the abbey had just so happened to sink another well in the middle, but one that any traveler wouldn't see coming. So sure enough, in 1386 one traveler fell right down into it and drowned.

And then the abbot claimed all his money and possessions for the monastery.

Don't worry, though—not every hidden trap was malicious. Traveling through the Low Countries? That lovely dusting of snow on the road might disguise a ditch deep enough to bury a man and his horse alive. In this case, at least, the nearby abbey was less interested in stealing a traveler's money and more interested in claiming its abbot had worked a miracle to rescue the rider and look like a saint—

a saint whose reputation might bring the monastery far more money than the traveler carried.

(Don't worry. The abbot saved the horse, too.)

But you really don't want to blow your party's first dramatic rescue or tragic accident on a *ditch*. So it's good to know that Chertsey Abbey's failures to build and maintain roads were only lawsuit-worthy because roads in the Middle Ages were not usually so theoretical.

Given that your travel experience has been limited to not nearly enough trips between your village and a market town or a saint's shrine, you probably think there are three varieties of medieval road: dirty, muddy, and deadly. But with the growth of population and regrowth of trade over the course of the Middle Ages, it became increasingly necessary and increasingly profitable to improve road quality along more traveled routes.

Building up small barrows as a roadbed could help prevent the pond problem. If you were lucky enough to be Charlemagne around 800, you could order your underlings to travel ahead of you, smoothing out the road and trimming back tree branches just itching to smack you in the face. (You are not lucky enough to be Charlemagne.)

If the wheels of the (very) occasional cart created ankle-breaking ruts, the local landlord could lay wooden slats across the surface. Or they could just be the engineers of Marlborough, who made the roadbed wider each time it was too torn up. It eventually stretched nearly a kilometer across. That's some serious commitment to mud.

For the mud, just wash your clothes already.

You'll know when you're approaching a city when the roads start getting better. Western Europeans were already paving roads with tamped-down gravel in the high Middle Ages, and not just in cities. If you're really lucky, once in the city, you'll eventually get to deal with cobblestones. There was certainly no slog through mud in 1301 London, where a bystander yelled at Thomas atte Chirch for riding too fast.

Pro tip: Don't mess with premodern road rage. The pedestrian ended up dead, and Thomas ended up with a very good reason to be at church.

Meanwhile, the Arabized cultures of the Near East snorted at European "pavement" and "wheels." They took their cue from the Berbers powering the gold and ivory trade from and to Mali and switched from dealing with cart-drawing-oxen excrement to goods-carrying-camel excrement. (Arab and European sources alike are oddly silent on comparative poop studies.)

Essentially, people across the medieval world were excellent at adapting roads to meet their living and traveling needs, and subsequently adapting their living situations to match road conditions. Peasants preferred to live in central villages instead of isolated farmsteads in order to limit road maintenance; the Sámi people of northern Scandinavia trained reindeer to pull sleds. Berbers rode camels, Nurembergers laid cobblestones, and some people just hoped you'd fall down a well. You'll want roads (or, rather, you'll want the bridges and mountain passes they lead to), and you'll have them.

Of course, you'll also pay for them. No city or lord or king is going to fling money at your travel comfort. Cities went about it simply enough— tax every resident worth taxing (probably about half the population), and tax incoming visitors even more. Lords, on the other hand, compensated for their road budget by erecting toll castles—often just a single tower—to ensure no traveler made it past a crossroads or over a bridge without paying up.

Did the system work? Well, consider the Alps.

In case you haven't been keeping score, the center of the western Christian world was Rome. Separating Rome from the rest of the Christian world were the Alps. With the need for speedy messenger service from Rome to everywhere and the heavy merchant traffic to and from urban Italy, there was no getting around it: you weren't going around them.

And it was the *Alps*. In 1480, intrepid German priest Felix Fabri described one section of a *well-maintained* alpine road as single-file, narrow, knee-deep mud covered in snow, with jagged rock cliffs on one side and sheer drop-offs on the other. (Admittedly, a worthy setting for your first dramatic rescue or tragic accident.)

When he made his second trip in 1483, however, Fabri got a most pleasant surprise. Well, first he was unpleasantly surprised when he had to shell out some major silver at a new toll castle. But after that, he was sharing a wide, only ankle-deep muddy road with carts and carriages! With occasional things resembling guardrails!

Duke Sigismund of Austria and Tirol, the road's guardian, had calculated that he could turn a profit by attracting increased traffic, and he sure knew how to accomplish that. He was rich enough to blast through half a mountain's worth of rock face—with gunpowder. No wonder Fabri had been so surprised to see a toll castle, since, after that much gunpowder, he'd probably thought the duke didn't have very much to compensate for.

HOW *to* TRAVEL

hen it comes to the fourteen miles of road and "road" between your village and the closest thing that resembles a town, you're the expert. As for the rest of the medieval world? Time to turn to the *real* travel experts to learn what to do.

❧ HOW TO TRAVEL AS A PAPAL MESSENGER

- ◆ Pros: Horses supplied. Fast travel. Familiarity with routes. You're getting paid.
- ◆ Cons: The Alps. In winter.

Moving on now.

❧ HOW TO TRAVEL AS A PILGRIM

From the Muslim hajj to Christians' journeys to local shrines, pilgrimage was probably the most characteristically medieval reason to travel. In the earliest Middle Ages, long-distance pilgrims had tour groups and kept travel diaries. By 1500, pilgrims still had tour groups and kept travel diaries—and they had guidebooks, hotel discounts, legal protections, blessed swords, and souvenirs. For pilgrims, all of these were useless without the mindset of prayer and devotion that transformed a physical journey into a spiritual one. For you, they make it the perfect disguise.

Blend In by Blending In.

A pilgrimage could take the form of nearly any mode of travel. The ideal Christian pilgrim traveled alone, in prayer and meditation; the prudent pilgrim traveled in a group, to prevent bandit attacks. The exemplary pilgrim walked the whole way; the pragmatic pilgrim wore shoes they could afford to repair along that way; the lucky pilgrim had a horse. Most pilgrimages were short, usually a day's travel from the city walls or less. But a truly ambitious Christian might walk from Poland to Rome, a Jew might travel from Aragon to Jerusalem, and a Muslim might even cross the Sahara. It would not be suspicious at all for someone to see the same pilgrim on the road for days on end.

Weapons had their place at a pilgrim's side. By the twelfth century, priests offered blessings for the swords of travelers casting their pilgrimages as devotional Crusades. (The Church often cast the Crusades as militant pilgrimages.) One anonymous French pilgrim passing through Jaffa around 1420 grumbled about the additional fee he had to pay to carry his sword, while another remarked approvingly that Christian and Jewish foreigners were even allowed to carry weapons.

Blend In by Standing Out.

By the later Middle Ages, artwork and advice for pilgrims had developed a sort of uniform. Durable shoes, of course, but also a heavy cloak, a purse, a walking staff, and, most important, a wide-brimmed hat. The hat was practical, but it was also the place to display little badges from earlier trips. They weren't just souvenirs; they were tangible remnants of the benefits of the saint or the site, a material connection to the divine. Someone looking at a pilgrim wouldn't see the person, just a standard pilgrim. Someone looking closely at a pilgrim was likely just trying to see if they could outbadge them.

And when a pilgrim stood out because of their badges, it could help solve the biggest travel problem of all: funding.

We can't all be Bishop Gunther of Bamberg, whose garments were so over-the-top and opulent that he was mistaken for a king in disguise during his 1064 stay in Constantinople. And we can't all be the Jerusalem-bound pilgrims who rented feather beds in Venice for their voyage across the Mediterranean. (Shipwrecks and pirates? Bring it on. Uncomfortable nights? Never!) Ordinary pilgrims still had significant advantages over the business traveler.

Even local pilgrims in the earliest Middle Ages could take advantage of laws requiring shrines to offer overnight lodging. It was provided in exchange for a donation to the host monastery or chapel, of course, but that also brought with it hopes of a miraculous cure or early release from purgatory. And the spiritual benefits of pilgrimage didn't have to wait until after death, either.

Late medieval Christians found the dangers and difficulties of pilgrimage a fitting way to do penance for their sins. They also served as a hope for miracles, and Christians could also satisfy their emotional yearning to be close to the remnants of God's saints on earth. And they could expect a landscape of ever-proliferating shrines to help them out in this life and the next.

More pilgrims were advantageous for towns, because it meant more money spent by pilgrims. More shrines were equally advantageous to the pilgrims who were spending that money, because it meant more places competing for said money. The knowledgeable penitent could plan their journey through towns that offered pilgrims the medieval equivalent of hotel discounts and free parking. Tolls to cross that bridge controlled by the convent, or taxes to pass through the city gates? Those were easily waived by monks and magistrates. Within cities, inns undercut each other's prices for a bed and beer.

Flirting with the barmaid was not included, so don't even try.

This All Seems Too Good to Be True.

Often, yes. The existence of legal protections, like guaranteed lodging, did not mean that every shrine site cooperated with said decrees. Even in a scrutinized city like Rome, the wealthiest pilgrims still found themselves reduced to camping in tents during the jubilee year of 1300. The growth of the pilgrimage industry necessarily paired with the growth of an industry to extort and scam pilgrims, not to mention eager pickpockets at all those free or discounted inns. And for long-distance pilgrims, there were still the Alps.

But worst of all, the creeping fear inside every pilgrim's mind was the possibility of failure. Would-be mothers on the road to Conques cradled their stillborn infants to their chests, already praying to its patron St. Foy to return their children to life just long enough for them to be baptized. But sometimes, a saint looked the other way. In 1272, inseparable pair Nicole and Contesse made their painful way from the slums of Paris to the shrine of St. Louis at St.-Denis, hoping desperately for a cure to Nicole's sudden paralysis of speech and body. They stayed and prayed for nine days—but Louis and his shrine remained silent.

Plenty of priests taught pilgrims how to act on the journey there. But who taught pilgrims how to journey home after *that*?

This Is Too True to Be Good.

Nicole and Contesse, desperately poor to begin with, gave up nine days of Contesse's income to beg for a cure. People in the Middle Ages *believed* in the power of pilgrimage and its destinations.

Most of the time.

If "pilgrim" makes a good disguise for you, it makes a good disguise for anyone—and medieval people believed that, too. Bernard of Clairvaux (1090–1153), himself a miracle-working saint, groused about pilgrims interested in seeing everything in an exotic location *except* the shrine. By the fifteenth century, European nobles assigned to pilgrimage as penance for their sins got in the habit of paying others to travel in their places. German nun Hugeberc recorded how Bishop Willibald of Eichstätt, heading to Jerusalem around 720, was just one person on a long list of pilgrims accused of espionage. Not much later, a thief named Adalbertus disguised himself as a pilgrim to case an abbey church, from which he intended to steal copiously. Beforehand, he used his disguise to obtain all the free lodging, food, and religious services he could want.

Which brings you to one final option for travel:

❦ HOW TO TRAVEL AS A BANDIT

That's cheating.

HOW *to* STAY CLEAN

egardless of gender or skin color or possibility of being an elf, you and your traveling companions will definitely have two things in common. First, all of you are going to get terrifically dirty and sweaty on the road. Second, all of you have noses.

In 1638, English philosopher Francis Bacon proposed one way to reconcile those two characteristics in a book aptly titled *The History of Life and Death*. He advised his readers that it was better for one's health to bathe in the blood of infants than to drink blood out of a young man's arm. But he added that people (except kings, *supposedly*) tended to object to this. So perhaps you, gentle reader, might simply place something cold on your chest.

His advice did not mean Bacon was opposed to bathing in simple water. Just, as soon as you finish, you should immediately lather your body with liquid oil mixed with herbs.

Perhaps you shouldn't heed the thoughts of a man named Bacon on the myriad health benefits of animal fat. So, it's a good thing it's not 1638! People in the Middle Ages were plenty interested in the connection between cleanliness and health. If you're going to spend three months on a galley with 150 men who spend their days rowing, you'll start to agree. And you'll want directions for getting clean.

Immediately.

 THE SCOPE OF THE PROBLEM

"Large hail, polluted rain, and snow pour down through the polluted air. The earth stinks when it receives this." Sound like the days you spent in coal-burning London? No, that's how Dante describes the third circle of hell.

Oops.

As for the entrance to the fourth circle? "And there, because of the excess of stink emitted by the wide and deep abyss, we took ourselves behind the cover of a large tomb." And so the *Inferno*'s narrator, who later descends from the eighth to the ninth and lowest circle without pausing (except to be wrong about the identities of the damned), can handle all the sights and fear of hell—but tries to hide from the stench.

But hell was not to be out-smelled. In 1087, thieves attempted to carry off the body of St. Nicholas from Myra to their hometown of Bari on the Italian peninsula, in this case probably to bring their city prestige. However, they should have remembered that a pleasant-smelling corpse could be proof of sanctity. Once removed from its tomb, the saint's body gave off such a wondrous aroma that the people of Myra equated it with the odor of heaven. The tale grew in the telling, and by the fourteenth century, the scent had been so strong that it wafted all the way to the ships in the harbor.

Unfortunately for the Bari gang, the people of Myra also figured out that the lovely smell was the result of the body of their precious saint being freed from his tomb. By thieves from Bari. Oops. The example of St. Nicholas proved that cleanliness wasn't next to godliness, it was the *weapon* of godliness.

But how much you regret your failure to have soap isn't a hazard only because of ickiness. Lacking germ theory, medieval medicine held that disease spread through bad air. So when you finish your quest and win a castle (and possibly a princess), follow the example of Constance's Bishop Otto III von Hachenburg (who did not win a princess), and make sure at least one of your castles has a very isolated latrine tower.

And keep yourself clean, for heaven's sake.

 YOUR LAUNDRY

You dressed for fighting evil, yes. But did you prepare for fighting evil two—or three—days in a row in the same outfit?

Depending on how poor your village is (was), it might have been your only option. Tax exemptions show that half of all Londoners in 1338 probably owned two sets of clothing (or at least, it was considered realistic to claim so). Wealthier urbanites were not safe, either. Clothes were a popularly targeted item of home burglars, since people often sewed their money into their clothing for security.

So yes, you'll have to take some time to wash your clothes. For the most part, the basics of doing laundry don't change from era to era. You really only need a running body of water and so forth. The biggest issue for you is more that you need to do said laundry, and you need to find the time to do it. But whereas your village probably had a nice little creek, a productive well, or a surprisingly fancy irrigation system somewhere in the area, larger towns and cities faced additional problems.

In the 1410s, a small women's convent upstream of the German town Reute housed a very special living saint. Elisabeth Achler's miraculous, very visible stigmata bled—in abundance. So every day, her sisters carried her clothes and bedclothes down to the creek to wash. The bloody wounds might have been pleasing to God, but their result sure wasn't pleasing to the residents of Reute—whose clothes were getting bloody instead of clean.

Still, if you're worried about doing laundry, you'd do well to invite Achler along on your quest. She solved the town's problem by identifying a spot in the convent courtyard where they could dig a well. That's the kind of skill you need to conquer household chores.

And you could probably also use the help of those other sisters who kept doing her laundry.

Every day.

YOUR TEETH

You probably still have teeth.

Tooth rot and loss was less common than you might think in the Middle Ages. (Never mind that in the late Middle Ages, "honeycake-baker" was a recognized profession in Bavarian cities. Never mind that some medical texts advised cleansing your teeth with red wine.) However, the all-consuming agony of toothaches and abscesses were ever-present, meaning that medieval dentists were always in business, and they had more or less the one skill you'd expect.

But you *do* still have teeth that you'd like to keep, and you're not helpless. Medieval medicine recognized a rudimentary concept of toothpaste. In the twelfth century, one Italian physician recommended rubbing your teeth with walnut shells three times a day—this, they (and yes, there's a decent chance this author was a woman) added, would make or keep teeth white, not just clean.

This concept took on another purpose and vastly more urgency in the fifteenth century, when Portuguese doctor Gabriele Fonseca advised scraping your teeth with rough fabric, followed by a good dousing of pleasant aromatic spices, which was meant to fight the bad air in the mouth that caused sickness. The far more important result was fighting bad breath.

Too bad you can't afford spices.

Too bad your traveling companions can't, either.

 YOU

Among medieval Christians, not bathing was reserved for saints. Body odor represented the ability to transcend the desires of the body (such as not stinking) to focus on heavenly goods. You, however, are not a saint. About which your traveling companions are very glad, I might add.

Because most Christians in medieval Europe were also not saints, the late Middle Ages witnessed a revival of the old Roman tradition of public baths. The Islamic world needed no such revival. With cleanliness woven into Islamic precepts, many Muslims considered the foundation of new baths or the support of existing ones to be charitable donations.

The extent to which baths qualified as religious institutions was questionable. In Iberia, Christians owned baths that were run according to Islamic regulations, and rabbinical writers constantly scolded Jews for sharing bathhouses with Christians and Muslims. Comic poetry snorted that people emerged dirtier than they entered, metaphorically because of gossip, as well as sweat and other people's grime. Arab travel writers observed or invented exotically fanciful baths in faraway cities as entertainment and not a little bit of propaganda. In Baghdad, claimed one, there was a Moroccan bath where you would get *three towels* (how wasteful), but not a waist wrap (how nudist).

Wait! What about getting clean? Baths are about getting clean, about removing dirt and stench both symbolically and physically, although the physical ways probably mattered more to most people. Twelfth-century abbess and prophet Hildegard of Bingen went so far as to suggest that natural hot springs were heated by the underground fires of purgatory, cleansing bathers' souls as well as their bodies.

Except, perhaps, for the baths that went coed. And not in the "separate rooms" sense.

As for that . . . we'll just say that the increasingly shrill pressure on governments in the sixteenth century to close western European bathhouses coincided with the spread of syphilis.

❦ THE MOST IMPORTANT THING OF ALL

We've already observed that Arab (and all other) travel writers exaggerated or invented differences between their homes and destinations. However, your skepticism of their accuracy does not eliminate the fact that the writers had to be able to conceive of the foreign and exotic in the first place. Take ninth-century merchant Abu Zayd al-Sirafi (who was a real person, although he borrowed much of what he wrote from earlier authors). On the differences between Persia and China, he wrote, "The Chinese are unhygienic, and they do not wash their backsides with water after defecating but merely wipe themselves with paper."

Toilet paper. Abu Zayd is talking about toilet paper.

So there you have it. You need to wash your clothing, you should probably give up on trying to have good breath most of the time, and it would be a good idea to visit a bathhouse every chance you get. But the most important decision of all comes down to water versus paper.

Because in the end, how to keep the rest of you clean doesn't matter if you don't also clean your end.

WHEN (NOT IF) BANDITS
ATTACK YOUR PARTY

I t was the heat of summer 1493, and the Glowaty brothers had a grudge. To prove it, they took an entire town hostage. Bandits in the Middle Ages did not mess around.

But they're pretty eager to mess around with *you*.

The wealthy Slovak town of Bardejov was pretty good at what it did, too. New bandits were always prowling around—towns, villages, roads, castles. In the anarchy of the Polish-Hungarian border, towns were often left to defend themselves. And in this case, practice does make perfect, because by summer 1493, Bardejov had captured and promptly tortured four members of the Glowaty gang. One received the swift death of beheading, while three more hung from the gallows.

Fedor Glowaty was not amused, especially since one of the men executed was his brother. So the bandits took Bardejov hostage. *Deliver 400 gold pieces*, they threatened, *or we will burn your town and put your people to the sword. You and six other towns. Leave the money at one of these two monasteries and walk away.*

Bardejov did not leave 400 florins at Mogila or Leichna or any other monastery for that matter. In fact, its leaders let others do all the paying. Annoyed local nobles hired posses who drove the Glowaty gang to Poland. There, the even more annoyed nobles of Kosice had to hire an entire company of mercenaries to eliminate the legendary bandits.

Banditry in the Middle Ages was not always so dramatic, and it was never romantic. Not for you as the victim, and not for the "noble" thieves of the forest, either. People were arrested for stealing yarn, clothing, even salted fish (the protein bars of medieval Europe). Items like these weren't trivial to the people who would risk death by hanging for even the negligible sale price of yarn, or for something to eat during a long winter. The goods sure weren't trivial to their victims, either. Nor were the robberies that easily turned into murders—always a risk with people who had, metaphorically and literally, nothing to lose.

You'll probably have to cross large swathes of territory where attacks by roving robbers aren't exactly mundane, but also should not surprise you when they happen. (You're a hero. They will happen.) In the Near East, the passage across the Sinai Desert was essentially open season on rich pilgrims heading for Jerusalem. Across Europe, soldiers suddenly dismissed from an army after a truce were more or less assumed to be bandits in the making. In 1434, a group of six peasants in Burgundy even used "But they *could* have been bandits" as an excuse to murder and rob two ex-soldiers—a motive judged fully legitimate by all. Jewish rabbis debated the ethics of purchasing back your own stolen goods. And in 1474 Poland, one priest was shocked—*shocked*—to discover that his newly purchased hymnals and Eucharist chalice had been stolen from another church.

But sometimes banditry *was* that dramatic, even when Glowatys weren't involved. For example, those hundreds of mercenaries supposedly required to capture the gang needed *some* way to get more money after they spent that particular payout. Or just "England in the early fourteenth century," really. Forget those two monasteries that may or may not have been cooperating in the blackmail of Bardejov. In early fourteenth-century England, Robert Bernard, priest and occasional professor at the University of Oxford (really), embezzled money from his parish and got kicked out . . . and to get revenge, hooked up with a well-known outlaw gang. In 1328, a handful of its bandits invaded Bernard's former church, beat up its remaining vicar, and stole the most recent donations. Meanwhile, Bernard himself was already hard at work in a second parish, both in terms of being its priest and in terms of stealing from its own donations.

Early fourteenth-century England also contained Sir (yes, Sir) William

Chetulton, of Baddington and Broomhall in Cheshire, who was accused in 1320 of robberies and assaults around Acton. He made up for it by serving King Edward II in his war on rebels from 1321 to 1325, during which Chetulton turned himself and the king a handsome profit by looting their lands. In spring 1327, he received a royal pardon for whatever he had done prior to leaving the king's service and was promptly accused of six murders. At some point after that, he . . . the records aren't clear exactly what he did, but he wasn't caught, and so was declared an outlaw. In the spring of 1332, he turned himself in anyway, probably to have his outlaw status revoked so he could then be pardoned for *those* crimes by the summer. At which point he was assigned to pursue and arrest other robbers, a task at which he lasted all of two months before being accused of robbery and rape. Remember, this was *Sir* William Chetulton.

Or maybe you'd prefer the story of Sir Robert Ingram, who joined a bandit gang that included robbers, counterfeiters, and straight-up murderers—but still represented his city and region in Parliament. Because he was the mayor of Nottingham and the sheriff of Nottinghamshire.

Fortunately, you won't have to be on constant watch for nobles robbing for the fun of it or for the desperate bandits of the highways. Unfortunately, you'll need to be aware that with every new step, you might be walking into a war zone.

"Robbery and devastation of land" was a universal war tactic in the Middle Ages. It was cunningly cruel: ruin the enemy's territory and thus starve the soldiers otherwise. The soldiers would all be forced to participate in stealing food from the enemy's peasants (and their own monarch wouldn't have to spend money). It was also the standard means by which the larger kingdoms of medieval Europe—you might know them as France, England, and Germany—conquered land and consolidated power. Without customs and border guards, lords built networks of small castles and sent out regular raiding parties not just to keep their victims in line, but also to keep other lords away.

And don't go thinking towns kept their hands clean. Bardejov's town council received any number of requests from neighboring towns for the return of stolen horses. In 1456, Bardejov "arrested" two nobles and two burghers to extort a solid ransom for themselves. In 1479, the Hungarian king himself demanded that Bardejov pay up for its militia's crimes.

Bardejov, it turns out, was a little *too* good at what it did.

To summarize: in order to avoid bandits, you need to avoid roads, forests, deserts, shires, cities, and kingdoms. Good thing you have that armor.

HOW *to* CROSS
a CURSED SWAMP

he upside here is clear. You don't really need any special lessons to learn how to cross a cursed swamp. You've got the basic supplies already: knee-high boots with no holes in them, that wide-brimmed pilgrim hat, an exorcist. You just need to know what you're up against.

The downside is you also don't need to study cursed swamps to learn how to cross a cursed swamp. Yes, that is a downside. Welcome, my friend, to the world of late medieval toilets.

🪷 PUBLIC TOILETS

Yes, really, they existed. Some of them even had names!

If you're in Exeter, England, in 1470 or so, you can pay a visit to the "Pixie House." Its users had a better sense of sarcasm than the Londoners who dubbed their version the "Longhouse." On the other hand, the Londoners whose Longhouse had 128 stalls (yes, actual stalls) possessed a far better toilet building. Those Londoners could also pick and choose their favorite public latrines, which were scattered throughout the city. London was *committed* to its toilets.

It's probably a shock to learn that the experience of using an urban public toilet will be more or less the same as the latrine in your yard back home: over a hole while sitting on a wooden or stone bench. Cleaning off afterwards is a bring-your-own-rag affair. And the equivalent of modern flushing is the distance between the seat and the gutter or cesspit beneath. On the plus side, women can flush any feminine product they want to!

People had every reason to use the public toilets—even peer pressure. "Pees in the street" became a personal insult, or something only a *poor person* would do (. . . according to rich people). Incentive to maintain the latrines took a little more collective effort. The best strategy, in the end, was to convince rich people that donating money to maintain them was a great thing to put in their will.

❦ PRIVATE TOILETS

The advantages of private toilets stretched high as a latrine tower and deep as a cesspit. There was no putting up with other patrons. No dealing with winter, no dealing with Scottish weather ever, no getting robbed on the way to or from a public privy at night. Private toilets were more or less limited to people who could afford a yard for building an outhouse. But for their owners (and people walking by in the street, who were not getting buckets of urine dumped on them), domestic latrines were a great thing. Most of the time.

The inescapable consequence of owning or renting a toilet was the cesspit underneath. The inescapable result was the smell. The inescapable truth was that cesspits don't eliminate the problem of waste removal; they just delay it.

The typical solution was to follow the lead of public toilets and hire—or in fifteenth-century Nuremberg, your taxes would allow the city to hire—professional latrine cleaners. They were paid well enough to compensate for the danger and the social stigma of the job, too, and more importantly, to ensure they were good at their job.

The lesson here? Paying taxes is pretty much the easiest way to reverse the curse of waste disposal.

If you were lucky enough to situate your privy over a small stream or even a sewer, the easier waste disposal might help with the smell. But even then, you've still got neighbors. There was a good chance someone downstream was dumping enough to block up the whole thing and turn your latrine into a surprise fountain.

Remember, though, bad neighbors are bad neighbors, not a curse.

One final note: Like cities and individual donors, you'll want to spend money on keeping your latrine in good shape. Richard le Rakiere could tell you why. On August 10, 1326, he was sitting innocently upon his toilet when the rotted boards finally broke under his weight. He splashed down into the sewage.

Okay, now we're getting somewhere. About that curse . . .

✿ CHAMBER POTS

Well, Richard might disagree, but technically, in his example, we're dealing with his laziness rather than an actual curse. Which brings us to the "swamp."

Public toilets meant dealing with weather, inconvenience, and the public. Ergo, private toilets. Private toilets were expensive; ergo, chamber pots. Chamber pots; ergo, emptying chamber pots. Emptying chamber pots; ergo, windows.

If you decide to travel as a pilgrim, be absolutely sure to grab your wide-brimmed hat.

✿ SEWERS

So, medieval engineers were great at designing hydraulics. Custom irrigation systems to suit the climates of Yemen, Egypt, Germany, Spain? Done. A Southampton, England, pipeworks system from 1420 that was still supplying water to the city in 1800? Coming right up. It seems reasonable that the people so good at water supply would put their efforts to work with waste removal. And in fact, they did! But here, well . . . gold star, Middle Ages, you tried.

The technology for legitimate sewers absolutely existed and was put to good use. In England alone, one York monastery built an underground, stone-lined sewer that flowed into the nearby river. By 1300, Westminster Palace had managed multiple underground sewers. But London itself, so proud of its public toilet network? Not so much.

On the other hand, London had its reasons to reject sewers. Municipal sewers couldn't serve as *public* sewers—there was no way they could ever be big enough or flow fast enough to deal with a large population. People turned municipal sewers into public ones anyway, with results as—finally—swampy as you might expect.

But there are more tactics to try! Don't let that "swamp" become literal!

By the late Middle Ages, cities were digging gutters alongside their roads. They also redirected the "natural" "streams" underneath the luckiest latrines to weave among buildings and empty into a nearby river or lake. But here, too, cities faced a no-win situation. Build stone vaults above the channels, so as not to have open sewage flowing through yards and beneath buildings? Or leave them open, and also be able to safely channel rain, melting snow, river floods, and at least some of the chamber pot problem?

"A" for effort, Middle Ages, you really did try. You managed to keep the term "swamp" strictly in the realm of the metaphorical. Barely, but you did it. And "curse" has been well established as a metaphor. So much for learning the ins and outs of a cursed sw—

☙ GHOSTS

Paschasius was a fifth-century deacon in Rome, well known to be a good man. Unfortunately, he supported the wrong papal candidate in 498, and never asked God's forgiveness for his position. So, if you go to the bathhouse in Capua, you might see him there even today, his spectral form holding out a towel to serve you, trapped in his personalized purgatory.

If you'd rather avoid Capua altogether and go farther south to Tauriana, you don't have to worry about a deacon ghost popping up in the bath or toilet house. There are multiple attendants here, and they just act like they've worked here forever. Then again, there was that one time you brought along some precious religious relics as extra reward for the attendants' services, and one of them refused. Only a man living in the grace of God could even touch them, he explained, and he was neither in the grace of God nor living.

Sometimes, not even prayer can protect you. A young Franciscan friar was so overwhelmed by the power of God one day that he continued to pray and praise as he went to the privy. But when he was sitting down, cornered against the wall, a demon appeared out of nowhere. "You can't pray here," said the demon. "Filth is my domain."

So to summarize: Swamp, metaphorical. Curse, literal.

HOW *to* BEFRIEND
the ENCHANTED FOREST

aybe the Lady of the Lake is sitting under a tree when her magic spell entraps Merlin forever. Or maybe she uses the tree in her magic spell that entraps Merlin forever. Or maybe she outright entraps Merlin in a tree. Forever. Version after version of the Arthurian saga agrees—even the world's most famous sorcerer should never have set foot in an enchanted forest.

This legend is a big problem for you. Right now, you're taking a sunny stroll with a sultan through the gardens of his beloved vacation home, and you've wandered into a lovely grove of date trees and palm trees.

Except these trees are gold, or silver, or copper, and the figs are jewels. The palm fronds themselves are real, but sprays of water sprout from the branches along with the leaves. And the birds perched in the trees are silver and gold, glinting in the sun. The artificial birds open their artificial beaks to chirp a song that sounds anything but artificial, and then close their beaks. Other shining metal birds peck at the same piece of sparkling gemstone fruit—over and over and over.

Robots. You're pretty much standing in a forest of robots.

The Middle Ages have just levelled up, and you're going to need a new skill set to befriend this particular enchanted forest.

🌸 STRATEGY #1: BE IMPRESSED BY IT

The deeper in you go, the more the air sparkles with magic. On the outskirts, giraffes and elephants peek out at you from behind trees and inside clearings. Even the lions don't venture farther toward you, where the sun now glints off the gold dangling from the leaves of hundreds of palm trees, which offer all the juicy dates or ripe oranges you could want. But go in deeper still, and the trees grow gold and silver branches whose leaves flutter in a breeze that doesn't exist. The air is filled instead with the chirping of the silver and gold birds perched on its branches.

Finally, you enter the heart of the forest, the grand finale: in front of your eyes, a tree emerges out of the ground, already fully grown, with glittering metallic birds hopping about its branches. Even the gentle pools here seem magical, scented with roses and musk. So smile! You're . . . standing in the throne room of Abbasid caliph al-Muqtadir.

The animals that you—and more to the point, every outside visitor to the palace—saw were real, and so was the fruit you enjoyed. The gold birds, the silver trees, the perfume fountains, and the fluttering leaves were robots.

At no time should you forget the human craft that first gave them life. Every cranking of gears, every hiss of hydraulics or pneumatics reminded rivals of the caliph's wealth, power, and mastery over the workings of the world.

The strategy worked, too. Former Byzantine admiral Romanos Lekapenos led a diplomatic mission to al-Muqtadir's court in 917 and 918, and he sure saw the palace pleasure gardens. More than saw—wanted others to see, too. During his visit, Romanos was already in the process of staging a silent coup back in Constantinople. (As one does when one is in Constantinople.) Upon his return home, he seized power for real. And somehow, he still found time to write about al-Muqtadir's palace. Now *that* is an enchanted forest.

❦ STRATEGY #2: EXPAND IT

The mighty Byzantine Empire was not to be outdone by anyone. Forget animating the throne room. They animated the throne.

Romanos was eventually deposed and exiled by the same emperor he had once relegated to obscurity. (Constantinople at its finest.) But between his own coup in 919 and being subject to a coup in 944, he found engineers able to re-create and surpass what he had witnessed in the palace of al-Muqtadir. Shortly after Romanos's, shall we say, *departure*, Constantinople received an ambassador from Italy. The tree that greeted him in the imperial throne room was bronze, complete with chirping bronze birds perched on its branches. It (obviously) did not grow out of the ground. But the throne itself was flanked by gold and bronze lions. They opened their mouths each time they roared and beat their tails against the ground. Singing birds adorned the top of the throne. And this throne *moved*.

A foreign visitor would first encounter the emperor at almost eye level, the chair raised just a little to convey proper superiority. But when the ambassador rose from the standard greeting of kneeling to touch his face to the ground in respect, the emperor sat high above his head, as if flying.

Oh, and to make absolutely sure the visitor was the proper degree of impressed and humbled, as the ambassador prepared to leave, the lion would stand up and then crouch back down. The birds would go silent, but suddenly music would fill the air as if an entire orchestra were playing.

Again: robots. In the Middle Ages.

❦ STRATEGY #3: PUBLICIZE IT

Why sit back and wait for ambassadors to come be impressed? Medieval Muslim rulers made a near-habit of *gifting* wood and metal come to life to their western European counterparts, whose own automata were limited to the dreams of poets. In 807—almost *half a millennium* before the Latin west could engineer similar technology—an Abbasid caliph sent a Holy Roman emperor a water clock. Or rather: a water *cuckoo clock*. The hour was loudly announced by the clang of the right number of bronze balls against a basin, while being quietly announced by the appearance, and then disappearance, of the corresponding number of little men on horseback. That's just plain showing off.

Fast-forward to 1232. That year, one of the Ayyubid sultans sent Holy Roman emperor Frederick II a clock that had no interest in primitive earthbound material like water. It required its own tent, which is less extravagant than it sounds when you consider that people called it—really—a planetarium. And it contained the entire cosmos. The hours of the day were followed by the circular course of a model of the sun. The hours of the night were marked by the same trajectory of the moon.

In return, Frederick sent a white bear and a peacock.

❦ STRATEGY #4: MAINTAIN IT

Half a century after that diplomatic gift exchange, western Europe was finally smart enough to build its own automata. In 1302, Countess Matilda of Artois and Burgundy inherited a lavish garden that seamlessly blended natural and mechanized wonder. Living birds mixed with mechanical ones. A small river flowed lazily through the park, pausing to power multiple fountains. People could cross the river on a bridge adorned with moving, fur-coated monkeys. Or they could dine among the marvels in sunlight-filled buildings. But by the time Matilda took possession of it, things were starting to fall apart.

Matilda mobilized. And just as importantly, she had the money to back it up. Only two years after she took possession, the monkeys' fur looked like new again. The fountains eventually faltered, but soon splashed down their water once again. By 1314, her metallic birds shone with fresh, thick layers of real gold. Artificial and natural sounds filled the air.

Make no mistake, automata could still represent political manipulation and posturing. But Matilda spent more and more time at this particular palace, marveling at its wonders and adapting them to her own delight.

Like how she had her engineers repair her monkeys by adding horns so they resembled demons. About that delight . . .

❦ STRATEGY N/A

Even if you aren't impressed by it, can't expand it, shouldn't publicize it, and don't want to maintain it, don't do the following. (And I don't mean making demons.)

The Ottoman Empire finished off the Byzantine Empire in 1453, and besieged Vienna in 1529. Then they . . . stopped. In exchange, more or less, the Holy Roman Empire (hereinafter "the Germans") had to pay the Ottoman Empire (hereinafter "the Ottomans") a bribe (hereinafter "a tribute") to stay put. And every year, the Germans paid their tribute partially in automata. Which the Ottomans unfailingly dismantled for their parts and melted down for their precious metals.

After a few years, the Germans started sending a clockmaker to Constantinople in addition to the automata, to make sure they still worked. The mechanical devices consistently arrived in perfect working order. And just as consistently, the Ottomans melted them down. As their rivals knew perfectly well would happen. The Ottomans believed human-crafted automata usurped the singular power of God. Their very existence was sacrilege.

So, with beautiful passive-aggression from all, the Germans kept sending automata. And the Ottomans kept destroying them. Magic, wonder, marvel? All silenced, all lost, by both parties. Premodern robots and their destruction were the snottiest of diplomatic weapons.

Automata did, technically, help prevent the exchange of cannonballs and bullets. They just kept the two enemies very, very mad. In case you were wondering—no, starting a premodern Cold War is not a good way to befriend an enchanted forest.

HOW *to* CROSS
the BARREN WASTES

I f there was one thing that Duke Philip of Burgundy loved more than betraying various allies during the Hundred Years' War and still winding up with the name "the Good," it was the Crusades. The official crusades may have ended centuries before his time, but Philip (1396–1467) was a dreamer. He idolized the Crusaders. He longed to lead his own crusade. He even gave his vow to crusade a special name: the Oath of the Pheasant.

So, when Philip sent a scout on, shall we say, an *intelligence-gathering mission* to Jerusalem, he picked Bertrandon de la Broquière, the best spy in the world. Thus, Bertrandon is likely your best guide to the barren wastes—and how to win the day when its hardy, crafty, and wise residents somehow still need your aid.

Bertrandon (d. 1459) knew there was one way to get to the Near East: the Mediterranean and then the barren Sinai Desert. He also knew there were two ways to get home. The first was back across the Mediterranean; the second was up through Syria, across the expanse of the Anatolian interior, and across the Balkans. Again and again, Bertrandon heard that you could take the overland route a thousand times and die on every trip. But Bertrandon was determined to take the thousand-and-first trip, living to tell the tale.

And when he arrived back in Burgundy, he wrote a lavish account of his trip and made sure multiple copies were made. So young hero, I advise you to pick up that codex of his *Le voyage d'outremer* and get to learning the secrets of taming the deserts and dust storms of the barren wastes.

☙ 1. Take Money

Crossing a desert? The first thing you're going to do is buy or rent a camel, which will make the trip far more comfortable for you. The second thing you're going to do is hire a guide whose caravans will offer some protection against bandits and getting lost. The third thing you're going to do is look at your camel and sigh, because you'll have to buy or rent a donkey from your guide, who won't take you along if you don't.

Crafty Bertrandon explained that he avoided this fate by appealing to the governor in Gaza, who of course decided in his favor. But then, to earn the extra money that he should have brought, Bertrandon sold wine to a local Muslim who could not legally buy it from another Muslim. It was a common practice, but it gave that first caravan leader a chance to have Bertrandon arrested and thrown in jail. This time, Bertrandon was saved not by himself but by a Christian slave trader.

The lesson here? Bring along enough money to avoid making enslavers the heroes of the barren wastes.

☙ 2. Hide That Money

Throughout his intelligence-gathering mission, Bertrandon was very careful to keep his money inside his clothing or sewn into it. (This strategy explains the fifteenth- and sixteenth-century epidemic of naked robbery victims around medieval Nuremberg, and probably other medieval cities.) It served him well at the Serdenay monastery outside Damascus. He entered its church to view an image of the Virgin Mary that was said to sweat oil. A woman flew at him out of nowhere and attempted to anoint him with what she hoped Bertrandon would think was the sweated oil. Bertrandon yanked himself free, not giving her the chance to pickpocket him or to entreat a "donation" for the anointing.

Don't let your purse become the barren waste.

☙ 3. Disguise Yourself

When Bertrandon's local friends, who were probably handsomely paid guides, handed him a set of clothing, Bertrandon never even hesitated. For example, on the trip from Damascus to Bursa, the stakes could not have been higher. Bertrandon temporarily joined a caravan bound for Mecca, which was . . . not a good idea for a Christian. His guide smartly dressed Bertrandon in a long white robe over dark pants, a turban, and a linen girdle. It was the clothing of an enslaved man, making him easy to overlook.

Bertrandon's periodic changes of clothing do suggest two important questions: How many sets of your own clothing will you need, and how are you supposed to do laundry in the middle of a wasteland? For some reason, Bertrandon's codex fails to provide answers to either.

❦ 4. STUDY THEIR FORTRESSES

Because the word "barren" in "barren wastes" deserves quotation marks, you should follow Bertrandon's lead in his careful observation and description of any inhabited or deserted fortresses. For example, guarding the strategically placed city of Damascus, there is a small castle on a hillside that is surrounded by a moat.

In the city itself, there was a centuries-old stone funduq that used to be the private home of a wealthy local named Bertok. When the brilliant Mongol ruler Timur conquered Damascus in 1400, he utterly devastated the entire city—except this funduq, around which he even placed a guard to ensure its protection from fires and looting. The locals apparently did not explain why Timur spared the building, but perhaps it had something to do with beauty. Bertrandon took special interest in noting the fleur-de-lis decorations carved into the exterior stone.

Does something seem a little bit . . . off . . . about Bertrandon's intelligence-gathering priorities? Take better notes of the land on your own trip, and maybe start taking some notes about the purpose of his *Le voyage d'outremer*.

♕ 5. MASTER LOCAL WEAPONRY

The gradual infiltration of gunpowder artillery into western European warfare created a race to possess better and better guns and cannons. As a proper spy, Bertrandon not only mastered Turkish martial technology but also ensured his employer would be able to replicate it.

In Beirut, Bertrandon witnessed a sunset feast that featured singing, wailing, and cannons whose artillery left fiery trails across the sky. He speculated on various ways the cannons might be used to kill people or to frighten horses (interesting priorities), and decided it was worth the risk and the money to learn to make them. He bribed the chief artillery-maker to reveal the ingredients and construction. Bertrandon acquired those ingredients, plus the wooden molds essential for the missiles' construction. As his book proudly declares, he brought them back to France with him.

What his book does not proudly declare is how he carried the molds from Beirut to Damascus, up through all of Syria, across Anatolia to Constantinople, across the Balkans to Vienna, and from Vienna across the Holy Roman Empire to the king of France. In fact, in his later catalogues of possessions and clothing, he never mentions the molds again.

It certainly seems like when it comes to weaponry, Bertrandon is more interested in literary flourishes than the actual weapons. No, his priorities are definitely not the priorities of the best spy in the world. But how can you have a heroic quest without some suspension of disbelief?

♕ 6. HEIGHTEN THE DRAMA

Despite the financial risks of a general monastery stop and the specific risks of a monastery in the middle of the Sinai, brave Bertrandon was determined to visit St. Catherine's. *Le voyage d'outremer* skims over two days of boredom on the way there when suddenly—out of nowhere—a meter-long beast burst onto the scene! The local guides shrieked. But it was the lizard who scuttled away and hid behind a rock. Bertrandon and his companions Andrew de Toulongeon and Pierre de Vautrei dismounted, and

86

the two French knights set off after the creature waving their swords. The beast, barely a handspan high *but a whole meter long, remember,* let out a terrified scream "like a cat on the approach of a dog" but *fearsome, you understand.*[7] The knights struck the creature on the back, to no avail! Its scales were like armor!

But somehow, Sir Andrew managed to find a weakness with his sword and throw the animal onto its back. He stabbed it with great gusto, finally killing the desert's terrifying spawn.

Only when the battle was done did Bertrandon pause to relate that his party was never in any danger, just, the Arabs were scared and the Europeans weren't.

The scene provides action, tension, and triumph. It uses the killing of a terrified animal to develop the heroism of western Christians specifically named, and the cowardice of eastern Muslims in general.

Bertrandon's "espionage report" would seem to have characters and a plot. Is your confidence in its usefulness starting to wane?

❦ 7. ADD A TOKEN FEMALE

What do you mean, "lack of women" is what's wrong? The con artist in the church at Serdenay was very clearly a woman.

Still, Bertrandon had made it almost all the way across Turkey when he just *casually* mentioned—for the first time in the entire book—that there was a woman traveling along with his party. The wife of Hoyarbarach received a letter that her father had died, and she wept excessively. Also, she was very beautiful, according to the man gazing at her.

What do you mean, that's not enough to make her seem like a real woman? Bertrandon even gave this character a developed inner life.

Still, our author also hastened to point out that in one stretch of isolated Anatolian mountains, there was a tribe of thirty thousand or so women who dressed just like men and wielded swords like men and in times of war

---

7   Bertrandon de la Brocquiere, *Le Voyage d'Outremer de Bertrandon de la Broquière*, ed. C. H. Schefer (E. Leroux, 1892), 22.

fought like men. See? The barren wastes don't just have women, they have *strong* women.

Maybe *Le voyage d'outremer* just has a plot.

❦ 8. SHOW OFF YOUR WORLDBUILDING

. . . But sometimes a plot has to wait while an author waxes poetic on the things that really matter: "The goats [of Antioch] are, for the most part, white, and the handsomest I have ever seen, not having, like those of Syria, hanging ears; and their hair is soft, of some length and curling. Their sheep have thick and broad tails. [The people] also feed wild donkeys, which they tame: these much resemble stags in their hair, ears, and head, and have like them cloven feet . . . They are large, handsome, and go with other animals."[8]

Because in-depth knowledge of livestock is exactly the information you need to survive your trek across the barren wastes.

You finally have your answer to the lingering question about *Le voyage d'outremer* itself. Bertrandon's book is not an espionage report. It's *Twilight of the Crusades, Book Three: Blade of Turks*.

But why shouldn't Bertrandon have written a fantasy adventure? He took his trip in 1432, when crusade was Duke Philip's dream, and gave whatever report he gave to Philip at the time. He wrote *Le voyage d'outremer* in the 1450s, when crusade was Philip's fantasy. The duke's crusading Oath of the Pheasant was just one in a long tradition of oaths sworn over birds—a long literary tradition, stretching back through generations of romances to early French legends of King Arthur and his knights. Philip in 1455 wanted a romance for an audience, and Bertrandon wrote exactly what 1455 Philip asked him to write.

And with *Le voyage d'outremer*, Bertrandon did indeed prove himself the best spy in the world (not to mention your best role model). By making himself the protagonist, Bertrandon focused his adventures of crossing

---

8 Ibid., 85–86.

the barren wastes of Sinai and Anatolia on one person, not on advice for an entire army. Even his exaggerations are useful. It's always better to be overprepared than overwhelmed.

So, if you've got some barren wastes to cross, put down your sword and pick up a copy of *Twilight of the Crusades, Book Four: Age of Goats.*

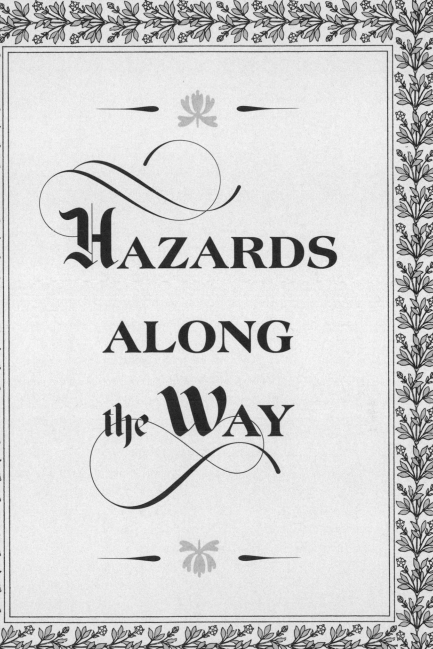

Hazards along the Way

WHEN *a* DRAGON ATTACKS *the* VILLAGE

t. George slew a dragon. Ho-hum.

St. George pacified a dragon by tying a piece of women's clothing around its neck, and then slew the dragon. That's better.

St. George saved a virgin from a dragon, pacified it by tying a piece of women's clothing around its neck, and then slew the dragon. Now that—that's *medieval*.

As medieval Christians told the story, St. George was traveling through Libya when he came across a city in mourning. A dragon had ravaged the city so badly and for so long that they had been forced to make a terrible bargain. When the dragon wanted, the town would choose a child or teenager by lottery and cast them outside the wall. A horrible death awaited the one in exchange for the temporary safety of all. And one day, the chosen one was the king's daughter.

The king is a stand-in for the mythical Israelite king Jephthah, who had been similarly tricked into sacrificing his daughter. The dragon is a stand-in for Satan. But the story nevertheless contains a compelling lesson: child sacrifice is a *really bad* way of saving your village from a dragon. (Take a moment to appreciate that your parents obviously agreed.) The Middle Ages responded much less murderously and more productively to the challenge faced by the legend's villagers. No matter how many times you've wished your village was dragon bait, you're a hero now, and heroes *save* villages. Even though you are neither mythical nor a saint like George, you would do well to learn from the legend's villagers how to handle the sudden appearance of a dragon in the sky.

✿ LESSON #2: DON'T PANIC

Remember *Beowulf*?

The Old English poem features three monsters that Beowulf has to face and defeat. Grendel attacks the mead-hall of Heorot, Beowulf's temporary home, because he is drawn to a world that had cast him out—which was not Beowulf's fault. Grendel's mother attacks because Beowulf killed her kid—technically Beowulf's fault, yes, but he had slain Grendel in self-defense.

Much like the first two monsters in *Beowulf*, the dragon is happily minding its own business until someone invades its home and steals one of its most precious possessions. So unless you're a greedy thief, the dragon probably isn't attacking your village in the first place.

✿ LESSON #3: PROTECT YOURSELF

The most important thing to know is that medieval dragons usually kill with venom, not fire. They breathe thick clouds of deadly smoke in all directions at once.

This is good news.

True, fighting fires has a more straightforward solution. Namely, buckets of water. But simple is not the same as easy—especially when those buckets of water needed to be filled and dumped by entire neighborhoods or even cities to have a hope of winning. If you have to deal with lizard halitosis instead, you're going to need a parallel example to help you prepare. You know what else features thick clouds of smoke spreading in all directions? Air pollution.

For some reason, the coal industry has never liked to advertise the fact that it got its jump start in the 1200s, particularly in England—and by the end of the century, Londoners were complaining about air pollution.

London's creative attempt to deal with the smog and soot from coal fires involved telling people to stop burning coal. This strategy was as ineffective for them as it would be for you if you tried yelling at the dragon to stop it.

93

So perhaps you could turn to the medieval experts on toxic smaug: blacksmiths! In 1473, a doctor named Ulrich Ellenbog offered smiths a foolproof four-point plan:

1. Cover your mouth with a piece of cloth.
2. Place good-smelling spices inside—medieval Europeans believed that diseases traveled in "bad air," so the best way to fight them was *good* air.
3. Because you also breathe in through your mouth, place beneficial items on your tongue. Beneficial, like cabbage or emeralds.
4. If all else fails: garlic and wine, my friend, garlic and wine.

✹ LESSON #4: HEAL YOURSELF

You might be out of emeralds, but you're never out of options! Make sure that in every town you pass through, the local apothecary is stocked up on theriac, the borderline miraculous powder that counters the venom of any deadly reptile (with one exception). Of course, theriac is made with ground-up *tyrus*, the skin of a snake found only in Syria (the aforementioned exception), which means the theriac you can afford is probably counterfeit.

Fortunately, even an era whose primary medical treatments involved leeches had its alternative medicine. So pack your bags for Italy! You can't miss the man standing by the city gates—a pitch-black serpent coiled around one arm, a viper curled around the other, a golden snake slithering around his shoulders. He is one of the "pauliani," named after the apostle said to be immune to snakebite. You can share in that immunity, he promises. All you need is a jar of St. Paul's grace . . . which you can buy from him. And only him. All the power of theriac for a much better price!

Did "St. Paul's grace" actually work? Well, consider that there are two types of people who never give up: heroes and swindlers.

HOW *to* SLAY *a* DRAGON

id you think you would learn how to slay a dragon from a book about etymology?

Because theologian and bishop Isidore of Seville's (c. 560–636) *Etymologies* is not ambiguous on teaching the matter. A wizard sneaks into the dragon's cave and sprinkles sleeping powder on the ground. Then they cut off the dragon's head while it can't fight back. Victory is achieved!

On the other hand . . . At this point, you know all about paying attention to the sources of what you're learning. Isidore's book is not about etymology in the sense of word origins. The *Etymologies* is an encyclopedia of everything in the universe, described by qualities supposedly derived from its name (but mostly derived from earlier authors). And Isidore's dragon-slaying advice is not about dragons. It's about rocks.

When discussing gemstones of fire, Isidore confronts dracontites: the glowing gem that is the pride of the kings of the east. Dracontites is found only inside the heads of dragons, but it will be nothing but an ordinary stone if you tear it from a dead dragon. The stroke that slays the serpent must reveal what is then a brilliant gem.

No matter how crushing it is, you've got to admit that there's a pretty big chasm between instructions for slaying a dragon and wordplay about a rock that doesn't exist.

When Isidore does get to dragons, he is more concerned with things like how dragons can slay you instead. (Be on the lookout for its tail suffocating you, like a boa. A boa that can fly.) The encyclopedia entry is not a total loss. Isidore's additional use of the common dragon versus elephant theme might suggest you should set aside your horse and ride an elephant into battle. He also says that dragons can live only in the tropical heat of India and Ethiopia. Slight problem. You've been to (or grew up in) Ethiopia, and the only dragons you saw were being slain by St. George in art.

To Isidore, on the other hand, Ethiopia and India weren't real places. They were half-mythical lands at the fringes of the known world, filled with marvels known and unknown. Half-mythical marvels like dragons.

No. That geography can't be right. Dragons *exist*. Why else would they be everywhere in the Middle Ages? You've never smelled the smoke of a dragon's breath. But you've seen plenty of them. They've glowed down at you from the stained glass windows of Cologne's synagogue, defiantly rebuilt after the pogrom of 1096. Or your fingers have brushed against sculptures of coiled dragons biting their own tails as you pass through city gates in 1200s Turkey. In the 1400s, dragon statues launched the rainbow of fireworks that began to explode across the skies of Europe.

And you've heard all about dragon *slayers*, too! (You don't even have to worry that Beowulf doesn't count because he was not a real person. In the story, he died. Anyway, he didn't slay the dragon. But nobody remembers that except the hero who actually *did* slay the dragon, in the end. And he can remember it because he did survive.)

No, recall when you dreamed yourself into the story of the greatest Persian hero, Rustam, who labored to slay a dragon with the help of his faithful horse Rakhsh. On a quest of his own, Rustam lay down for a nice little nap one day—right next to a dragon's lair. Rakhsh whinnied and pawed his sleeping master until Rustam finally woke up—and witnessed the dragon's angry, flaming arrival. The hero's tools (your tools!) were armor, a sword, and witty comebacks. As the dragon's tail began to coil around Rustam, he used his last moments of movement and breath to dart behind the dragon. Rustam stabbed and slashed at the dragon until the evil serpent lay dead before him.

Matters were somewhat easier in early medieval England. One medical charm suggested that it was the responsibility of the god Woden, or Odin, to slay the serpent by chopping it into nine pieces. Your responsibility was to neutralize its venom by mixing up a cure that included fennel, thyme, and crabapples. It's not quite as heroic to let a god do the slaying, but at least you'll get a snack along the way.

Dragons are everywhere; they must be. From India to Ireland, they're the ultimate embodiment of the primordial chaos that could engulf the world again, the alpha and omega of evil. They are . . . Wait, dragons are also demons. Or rather, demons are dragons.

Fortunately for all parties, a truly heroic quest requires you to slay a demon that's in dragon form. And you've got this one. If you're a medieval Christian, you know the story of St. Margaret of Antioch almost as well as the life of Christ. St. Margaret, who slew a dragon at the very moment when all hope seemed lost.

Margaret was the daughter of a fourth-century pagan Syrian who was raised instead by humble Christians. (In other words: Margaret was not a real person.) She was nevertheless set up to marry the king. (Definitely not a real person.) She predictably refused to give up Christianity and was thrown in jail. There, her predictably beautiful, virginal body underwent brutal tortures, but her faith never wavered.

But in the Middle Ages, that part of the legend could (and did) happen to any old beautiful, virgin, and apocryphal woman saint. Margaret, however, was the only one who curled up in her prison cell one day, in the middle of weeks of agony, when a dragon crashed into her cell, its claws extended and its jaws open wide like the mouth of hell. Its tail snatched her up and threw her into the infernal jaws.

Being eaten is not how this story is supposed to go.

Margaret had no armor, no sword. But she had the supernatural. She made the ritual sign of the cross: from the belly of the beast, she touched her forehead, the middle of her chest, one shoulder, the other shoulder.

And burst the dragon's stomach wide open in the world's worst case of indigestion.

But somehow, Margaret did not become the patron saint of the gastro-intestinal tract. Instead, she became one of the most popular and important saints all over western Europe for her healing powers in general—but especially for pregnant women and women in childbirth. Even the standard iconography of Margaret slaying the dragon resembled drawings of women undergoing cesarian sections.

Except—unlike for Margaret—C-sections were the absolute last resort in medieval childbirth. Almost without exception, they meant the death of the mother and probably her baby. The desperate hope was for the newborn to live long enough to be baptized.

So medieval mothers created a religious-magical ritual of their own. As they gave birth, surrounded by female relatives, they brought with them amulets with icons of Margaret or scraps of her biography. Margaret's defeat of the dragon was a "rebirth" that defeated her death. A rebirth that defeated the death of the new mother and her child.

And you know what? Medieval childhood mortality statistics were horrific—50 percent of children dead by age sixteen. For mothers, though? With the help of St. Margaret the dragon slayer, a future mother had around a 98 percent chance of surviving giving birth. Her life and her child's birth were Margaret's new life. Every time a woman gave birth in the Middle Ages, a dragon was slain.

Although it's probably easier to grab some armor and a sword.

HOW *to* TAME *a* DRAGON

aming dragons is God's will.

After all, as the Norse Christians insisted, how can you be a hero without it? Dragons are the most majestic creatures under the sky. Dragons can soar above the earth carrying a person in their claws or mouths gently enough to cause no harm. They can stop the attack of an enemy horde instantly, through emotion rather than slaughter. And when you inevitably end up in the villain's dungeon, they will light the way out for you. Which goes to show that binding the magic and majesty of dragons to your will might be the greatest power of all.

So what if those examples do not, technically speaking, involve a deity. No less an authority than Thomas Aquinas, one of the greatest theologians and philosophers of all time, knew beyond all doubt that taming dragons was God's will, and Christians had a duty to try. But how?

The story, as you might expect, starts with fan fiction.

Early and medieval Christians loved to write fanfic about their favorite biblical characters. Sometimes it even became canon. That process is how Simon and Jude, two of Jesus's closest followers, went from the Last Supper in Jerusalem to a palace in Persia, standing in front of the king with their lives on the line. The two men were exhausted. They had converted the entire kingdom and most of the king's court to Christianity. What more did God want?

The court sorcerers were in a foul mood of their own. They had just lost a debate with a team of lawyers about the supernatural, supposedly their field of expertise. As sore losers are wont to do, they un-leashed the snakes. One hundred slithering, deadly, *serpentes*.

Simon and Jude recognized this ploy. When God told Aaron back in the time of Exodus to throw down his staff, the staff turned into a bigger serpent and ate the others. But that day in Persia, God was silent, and the wooden staffs of Simon and Jude stubbornly remained wooden staffs.

If you can't make a snake, just take a snake. The two saints pulled off their coats, set them down on the floor, and allowed a mess of killer snakes to slither onto them. Simon and Jude flung their coats at the sorcerers and called on God to make the sorcerers stand still so they could be torn to pieces.

God listened and agreed, but apparently also reminded Simon and Jude that their actions were rather unsaintly. The pair took that to heart—listening to God is usually a good idea. Still, they waited a good while as the sorcerers begged for the mercy of death.

Finally satisfied, Simon and Jude commanded the serpents to slither their way out into the desert. No attempt to kill the snakes. No waiting for God to turn the snakes into wooden staffs. The saints sent the *serpentes* away, and the *serpentes* obeyed.

Centuries later (this time in real life) came Thomas Aquinas. En-sconced safely in a Paris university room, he read *everything* having to do with Christianity—the original Bible, the expanded universe, fan analysis after fan analysis. If there was anyone who should write the entire wiki, it was going to be him, and he called it the *Summa theologica*.

At one point in his writing, Thomas arrived at the part where he had to prove that people hoping to send away demons may call on God to give them the power of exorcism. A key intermediate step in this proof: proving that humans can command irrational creatures. Which is to say, animals. And of all the evidence he could provide to support his argument, Thomas picked the story of Simon, Jude, and the serpents.

Except for Thomas they were only serpents in the broad, "lizard" sense of the word. He read the story, memorized it, and in the *Summa theologica* offered his own spin: *dracones*. Which is to say, possibly *the* most important Christian theology book from the Middle Ages tells readers, unambiguously, that humans can, may, and should tame dragons.

There's just one small, almost trivial detail missing: how to actually do it. You might find something about training a wild beast in some codex or other, but the book was probably copied by a monk who has never seen anything more exotic than a mouse. Don't expect much help in dragon-taming methods from Christian writers outside the Church, either. Far too many noblemen wanted to prove their manliness by informing the world how *they* trained their hunting animals, but they meant dogs and falcons. Oh, but then leopards! Those same noblemen wanted to prove their nobility by showing off a pet leopard . . . leopards who were purchased *as* pets in Alexandria, where they had been trained by Muslim keepers. The elephant whose tricks so entertained fifteenth-century Venice, Germany, and France had sailed across the Mediterranean from its original trainer, too.

Fortunately, medieval Muslims did know how to bind dangerous, unruly creatures to their will. They were also willing to provide directions.

It's true that Muslim veterinarians' instructions focus on cheetahs, not dragons. But consider this: after Simon and Jude had mastered the taming of *serpentes*, they had to perform the same trick at another king's court—this time with tigers. If the story holds, God had already linked taming dragons with taming big cats. And why not? Taming cats takes patience and cheese. Taming dragons takes patience, cheese, and not stealing their hoards of gold.

Fourteenth-century veterinary expert Ibn Mankali, a name generally associated with naval warfare, offers a two-pronged program for building a friendship with your cheetah. A list of instructions is not proof that the instructions work (when I think of naval warfare, I always think of cheetahs). On the other hand, Ibn Mankali's instructions do list patience and food:

1. Restrain your newly captive cheetah completely while she is lying on her side, so the only thing she can move is her mouth.

2. Set down a bowl of cheese next to her head. First, she will lick the cheese, then eat it. (The existence of an intermediate stage seems ... less than realistic.)

3. Once she has eaten her fill of cheese, you step in: serve her small pieces of meat, one at a time, so she associates your presence with good food.

4. Bit by bit, allow her more freedom to move: to lift her head, to move her paws, to sit up, to stand up. But at each stage, only feed her each time she completes the newly allowed action.

5. It's kind of like positive-reinforcement dog training, except for the part where Ibn Mankali's end goal for cheetah-taming is to teach it to ride a horse.

Not sure you're up for the challenge? Maybe you just have a problem cheetah? The twelfth-century Syrian court is here to offer you some better ideas. Namely, bring in a woman to train her.

Such was the case with one sultan's favorite cheetah. The woman's name is lost to history, but her extraordinary friendship with this big cat is not. The trainer made a collar and leash to take the cheetah on walks. The cheetah even let her pet and groom it.

As if that wasn't enough, the trainer went further. She and the sultan cared enough for this cheetah to give her a velvet-covered straw bed. As the story goes, one day the trainer grew furious with her cheetah when the cat urinated on the velvet instead of off to the side. In short: she had litterbox trained a cheetah.

Litterboxes are surely not on anyone's mind when taming their first wild dragon. No, you likely envision yourself soaring across the sky, safely in its claws, or ordering it to light your way free of a cave. That's what heroes do. They don't make dragon bathrooms.

102

On the other hand, litterbox training is what will make you a hero to the people on the ground beneath the dragon, which can fly.

HOW *to* SURVIVE *a*
SEA MONSTER ATTACK

elcome aboard! Would you like to go to hell?

You were probably thinking the sea monster would be the easy part of the ocean leg of your quest. It takes (literal) miracles to save people from drowning in shipwrecks. Pirates will sell you into slavery, throw you overboard to drown, or murder you outright. In comparison, Nessie is kind of cute, and could make a good pet.

But you will pretty quickly have bigger things to worry about than death if that sea monster off your stern decides to take a bite of boat meringue pie. So yes, you should definitely worry about ancient Near Eastern and prehistoric proto-Indo-European primordial monsters of the cosmic ocean who must devour the world or die.

You may have been lucky enough to have laughed off this myth, thanks to an ancient Hebrew satire about a disobedient prophet who gets swallowed by a generic big fish. Medieval Christians observed that Jonah stayed eaten by said not-actually-a-whale (really—the Bible says nothing about a whale specifically) for three days. Hey, didn't Christ spend three days in hell between Good Friday and Easter Sunday? (Yes.) Aren't a mouth and being eaten near-universal symbolism for the entrance to hell and going there? (Also, yes.) So, Christians declared Jonah's adventure an allegory for the three days that Christ spent defeating the devil before rising from the dead. Okay, maybe Jonah fought stomach acid while Christ fought Satan. Their fights still took place on the same unholy battlefield. So if you get eaten by that sea monster off your stern like Jonah did, you're on your way to hell.

But if you want to avoid a simultaneously literal and metaphorical hellmouth, you're going to need every strategy you can gather, from Greenland tundra to European libraries to where there be dragons.

🪷 BAFFIN BAY

You were impressed that the Norse got into boats and sailed from Iceland to Greenland? In the twelfth century, the Thule made it there from *Russia*, and maintained open lines of communication and trade in pottery from Baffin Bay back to Alaska. The Greenland Thule and their Dorset predecessors (the Norse look less impressive by the minute) stuck around because they had the sea beast known as the walrus for a food source. Walrus meat was both easily accessible and more or less easily acquired. The Thule were also happy to adapt their walrus-hunting skills to the narwhal, a creature that Europeans as a whole viewed less than fondly (. . . and the Norse now look even less impressive).

But if trade goods are any guide, the Norse were mad for ivory. Walrus? Narwhal? Their trading partners smiled at the challenge. Where the Norse feared to sail and stab, the Thule faced down the creatures and won.

Unfortunately, unless you are Thule, cultural appropriation like "not being afraid" will probably get you eaten.

🪷 RED SEA

In the tenth-century book *Marvels of India*, Buzurg ibn Shahriyar explains how he learned to survive a sea monster attack from Muhammad al-Hassan ibn Amr, who in turn learned it from a sailor who survived an attack. I know, you have no idea who Muhammad al-Hassan ibn Amr is, and Buzurg ibn Shahriyar wasn't a real person . . . but you need *all* the strategies out there to stay out of hell. And the sailor in this story *won*.

Moving on. The nonexistent sailors were making their way up the very real Red Sea when a monstrous fish smashed into their hull so hard that they could have believed the ship dashed into a cliff. But it didn't sink! The truth was revealed once they reached the port. The smashed hull was sealed up by the severed head of the monstrous fish. It had gotten its head stuck in the side. And as it struggled to get free, a truly monstrous fish had swum along and had itself some nice sashimi. But the hole remained sealed by the remnants of the first sea monster.

This adventure unquestionably offers an example of how to survive a sea monster attack. A good example, though? Relying on a *deus ex beluga* is lazy and will probably get you eaten.

☸ JORDAN RIVER

Felix Fabri was a real person (1440–1502) who went to the real Jordan River (1480, 1483), wrote a real travel diary that was mostly true, and was skeptical of legends about the river that other travelers accepted as real. (He leaves it to the reader to decide whether a linen tunic washed in the Jordan will save you from arrows.)

Muslim tour guides at the river warned Christian pilgrims that swimmers would sometimes just . . . simply vanish, so they should under no circumstances swim across the river. But, of course, all the men did it anyway. So now you get to picture a middle-aged monk stripping naked (the swimsuit of medieval Europe) and frolicking in a river.

On Fabri's first trip, one of his fellow swimmers, indeed, simply vanished. The poor man finally resurfaced, unconscious and half-drowned. He vomited up the water he had swallowed and was able to tell his pitiful story. Something had brushed against his leg! And it was as if all the strength had left his muscles. He was being pulled down and down, and there was nothing he could do.

The question wasn't *whether* a sea monster had tried to drown him, but *what kind*. Fabri related the options he heard: (1) soul- and body-sucking creatures of the deep who lurk on the muddy river bottom, ready to rise up and *snap* at any human leg they see. (2) Beasts who swim up from the Dead Sea, in which nothing can live, as if swimming up from hell. (3) The water

105

itself was the monster—that bitter, bitter water of the Dead Sea pushing its poisonous way up the river.

Fabri the Dominican friar and theologian, however, felt compelled to turn the near disaster into a lesson. He tried to argue that the terrifying event was God's punishment for stripping naked and splashing about in the sacred river.

Waiting until the invention of swimsuits is certainly a *novel* approach to surviving a sea monster attack. But given the firmly medieval nature of your quest, it will probably still get you eaten.

✿ ENGLISH CHANNEL

Fictional or not, the tenth-century poem "A Certain Fisher Whom a Whale Swallowed" (plausible enough) featured an English fisher named Within (never mind the plausible part) who was, in fact, swallowed by a whale. Within was within for a terrifying five days, as he fought to free himself and his little boat. Slicing and hacking at the whale's stomach with his trusty sword, Within managed to drive the monster toward the shoreline and onto the beach. But he was able to kill the whale only when he set fire to his boat—while he was still trapped inside.

Within refused to be stuck within without a fight. He started yelling for help. The local villagers, who had arrived on the beach to carve up the whale for its meat, heard Within instead. They assumed the whale was possessed by a demon, lost their appetites, and ran away in fear. Eventually, though, they came back and turned Within into Without.

Starring in a poem called "A Certain Fisher Whom a Whale Swallowed" will definitely get you eaten. Bringing along a boat, a sword, a beach, and hungry villagers will help you survive being eaten. Making people think you're a demon will probably get you burned at the stake.

Next example.

✿ ALL THE WATERS OF ALL THE EARTH

Not scared yet? The Hebrew Bible describes the greatest ocean dragon of them all. His body is made of molten shields with no weaknesses, and his breath is fire. To him, swords are nothing but straw, and armor is made of rotten wood. God made him to be lord of the deep, mightier than the rest of creation. He was the "king over all the sons of pride."

But the medieval Jewish readers who understood that every single person was a child of pride found one story repeated over and over and over. At the end of days, God would slay the worst sea monster of them all, the most powerful enemy in all of creation. And at the final banquet, all of humanity would feast on its flesh.

The prophecy of the final feast resonates in the lives of the Jewish readers, Christian writers, Arabic tale-tellers, and Thule walrus hunters of the high Middle Ages. From the frozen shores of Greenland to the banks of the River Jordan, one truth shines forth: the way to avoid being eaten by a sea monster is to eat it first.

HOW *to* NOT GET EATEN

I t was supposed to be an ordinary Sunday. The French villagers in Sens crowded into their church that day in 858, women on one side, men on the other. The priest began the liturgy, in Latin, with his back to the congregation. The congregation was supposed to be standing still and facing the priest, but most of them were probably jostling around their side of the gender-segregated church, mingling and gossiping and being glad that pews would not be invented for centuries. Just an ordinary Mass for an ordinary day. Then a wolf burst through the doors.

The beast tore through the men's side of the church, knocking them into each other, sending them sprawling. It proceeded to race around the women's side, just as violently. And then it ran back outside, vanishing into the forest. In case you're not keeping score, the number of people killed by the wolf was zero. No one lost their life, a limb, or anything but time to gossip.

A happy outcome is almost unfair. As a questing hero with a party of traveling companions, you deserve to be scared of wolves stalking the woods alongside roads. Old Norse used the word *vargar* to mean both outlaws and wolves. *Vargar* attack and murder travelers all the time. Governments in France and England offered bounties on wolf hides in an attempt to wipe out the beasts.

As the years and failed Crusades roll on, you deserve to be getting more scared. A few centuries of population growth in high medieval Europe meant humans and livestock were invading wolves' space more and more. Wolves don't recognize a culinary difference between wild prey and flocks of sheep. No matter that all those wolfskin bounties drove wolves to extinction in some parts of Europe by 1500. A wolf still killed fourteen people outside Paris in 1438! All the chronicles say so!

Or you could interpret it as "A wolf killed fourteen people in 1438, and people talked so much about the event because attacks were so rare." And you'd be right. To provide a little more context, a devastating famine year in 1438 had driven wolves to attack people out of desperation. There's only one logical conclusion: the Middle Ages has had centuries of such lousy PR partly because they spent their advertising budget on slandering wolves.

Don't worry, though. You can still gain hero points by fending off animal attacks. All you need is a late medieval city that really likes bacon. It turns out that keeping a sow is a really great way to ensure your family has a supply of meat that isn't salted fish, and it's a lot more economical to let your pig roam the streets and eat garbage than to feed it yourself. The only problem was that wandering pigs had the bad habit of occasionally breaking into houses and eating babies. It was a big enough problem that city governments in Germany passed laws forbidding people from letting their pigs roam about. These ordinances were as effective as you would expect, which leaves ample opportunity for you to dash in and save toddlers from the jaws of pigs. And hey, not being eaten pales in comparison with not being eaten, plus bacon.

Oh, does killing a cute, intelligent pig make you kind of queasy? Or maybe you're a Muslim, a Jew who needs a kosher butcher, or a Christian during Lent who forgot to pay the Church to waive your fasting requirement? Or you're just cranky that killing a pig is not exactly the height of drama and fending off a dramatic wolf attack is not going to happen. Stop worrying about your hero cred. You're still in deep danger of being eaten, and not from any old animal skulking along a dark roadside. I am talking, of course, about the most dangerous predator of all:

 CANNIBALS

All the experts agree: Think twice before you set your course for the edge

HOW TO NOT GET EATEN

of the world. A storm might blow you off course to an island beyond even Sumatra. Its residents will eat you, and then put your skull on display like a trophy. That's not a possibility; it's a fact. And don't bother with a desperate attempt to get your ship back on the sea. You'll need to restock your ship with food and freshwater somewhere. And, well, all the islands on the fringes of the Outer Sea are peopled by cannibals.

But can you protect yourself from becoming ingredients if you do, in fact, end up at the end of the world? You can if you study the story of one tenth-century sailor who did, somehow, find a way to freedom.

On an unnamed island off Sri Lanka—cannibals near the known world! well, sort of—the cannibal king himself invited the sailor to dinner. It was a lavish feast—except for the entrée swimming in a sauce that contained chunks of head, foot, and hand. As you can probably imagine, the sailor was done eating for the night. (Maybe for many nights.) The next morning, as he prepared for a hasty departure, the cannibal king held out a fish. "This is what we eat," he told the sailor. "This is what you ate. The best of our fish." The supposed cannibal king was just pulling a prank? Well, that's a relief. Not being eaten is an unqualified good. And you can't be eaten by cannibals if cannibals don't exist.

So you can sit back, relax, and enjoy many, many more medieval tales costarring cannibal villains in deserts and on islands. Like the tenth-century Arabic story of *another* island somewhere near Sri Lanka, which is a triple snare from which no sailor has ever escaped. If you land on this island, you're devoured by tigers. If you're quick enough to jump off your ship into the water, crocodiles are waiting, and they are hungry. And why would you jump overboard? Because the pirates who just boarded your ship are going to steal it . . . and eat you.

Hold up. Cannibal *pirates*?

Okay. Never mind that this tale allows no way for a sailor to survive and tell his story. Never mind that "cannibals" are only ever seen eating fish. Never mind that cannibals always live at the edge of the world, which nobody has ever visited. There are *cannibal pirates*.

Wait, no. Being eaten is a bad thing. The best way to survive a predator attack is if there are no predators. So it's good that cannibal pirates don't exist in the first place.

What a bummer. Why should you have to defeat the hordes of evil to save a world that doesn't have cannibal pirates?

WHEN DARK CLOUDS
APPEAR *on the* HORIZON

hen dark clouds appear on the horizon at some point on your journey, there's no need for concern. Just hire a weather-wizard.

Yes, the Middle Ages had weather-wizards. They were called *tempestarii* or *tempestariae*, and they were the saviors of ninth-century France and England. When storms loomed on the horizon, *tempestarii* had the power to communicate with the clouds and force them to leave.

Sometimes weather-wizards were called *inmissores tempestatum*, which means "senders of storms," and they had the power to call down thunder and hail. They recited incantations to invite in storm clouds that destroyed peasants' harvests.

An important addendum: the *tempestarii* and *inmissores tempestatum* were the same people, and they wanted the same thing: your crops. All you had to do to make them stay good was give some of your harvest to them instead of to the Church.

Does *inmissores tempestatum* sound a little too elegant and grammatically correct for peasant sorcerers? Does the specification about paying them *instead of* the Church seem suspiciously precise to you? You really might be right. The early medieval Church liked to declare that *tempestarii* were sinners. Early medieval European governments, often prompted by the Church, occasionally declared that *tempestarii* were criminals. But somehow, the only *tempestarii* you'll meet in the literary sources that you might look to for guidance are not actually *tempestarii*. Rather the opposite.

Around 816, Archbishop Agobard of Lyon wrote down the story of his conversation with a man who claimed to have seen, with his own eyes, a *tempestarius* in action. It was a *claim*, Agobard assured his readers. He had talked the man into admitting he had not, in fact, seen anyone perform any kind of weather magic—that he had invented the story entirely.

On another occasion, the situation was far more dire. Agobard had chanced upon a posse of villagers. They were on the verge of stoning three men and one woman to death—right that moment. The villagers explained that the four people were cloud-sailors who had fallen out of one of their airborne ships. Agobard described himself reciting a long speech and having an extensive debate with the villagers, which he naturally won. They admitted their belief was wrong and freed their prisoners. This time, no suspected *tempestarius* or *tempestaria* was even involved.

Agobard, a tireless investigator and hero (according to his own account), found plenty of people who believed in the existence of *tempestarii*. But nobody was one. Nobody knew one. Nobody had even seen one. So good luck finding one to help with your quest.

But not to worry! The Middle Ages still had weather-wizards. Just, they were called saints and priests. With their incantations and ritual spells, they were the saviors of a lot more places than just France and England.

People in southwest France turned to priests to pray for enough rain for their crops, and priests held special church services to ward off thunderstorms. Priests in early medieval France and Germany (like, say, one Agobard of Lyon) were empowered by prayer to drive away thunder and hail. *How curious.*

When particularly bad storms arrived despite these attempts, people generally took shelter in sturdy stone churches. But who needs a building when you have a legitimate saint? As the story goes, an English-German missionary and abbess named Lioba (c. 710–782) stepped out into the worst storm the villagers had ever seen. She made the ritual sign of the cross— 113 raise one hand to your forehead, draw it down to your stomach, touch one side of your heart, trace it across to the other side. The storm evaporated instantly.

No need to worry that Lioba's hagiography only mentions one success. The chances of a hero like you encountering more than one severe storm are surely rather low. The story's lack of clear distinction between religion and magic isn't a problem, either; that's how medieval Christianity rolled. The problem is more that the man writing about Lioba needed some miracles to make her look like a saint. *Hmm.*

Fine. Other examples might still be called for to learn how to deal with those dark clouds on the horizon. How about a figure who challenged a rival sorcerer to a *weather duel*?

Hertigar was just an ordinary guy from Birka, Sweden, until he became the first person in his village to convert to Christianity in the ninth century. One day, right before a rainstorm, a group of men started making fun of him for being a Christian. Hertigar snapped right back that *their* gods couldn't keep the rain away, but *his* God could. Hertigar and the other men set themselves up on opposite sides of a forest clearing. They all began their chanting. The clouds opened up, and then the pagan sorcerers were utterly drenched while Hertigar stayed completely dry. Divine weather magic works.

However, Hertigar isn't a saint. So maybe saints can't be weatherwizards?

But don't worry! The Middle Ages still had weather-wizards. With the right tools, you can absolutely be one of them. You don't even have to join a (nonexistent) pagan sect or be (not) killed by Vikings to do it.

You'll find your most useful tool is a simple cross. You can plant a wooden one on a hillside overlooking your fields to keep away hail. Give this cross a special blessing, and it might even fend off early or late frosts. You can emulate non-saint Hugh of Cluny (d. 1109), who pulled off a Lioba when he made the sign of the cross gesture to drive off a similar storm. A *cynic* might suggest that early medieval priests stressed the quasi-magical power of the Christian cross in order to teach people the importance of Jesus's death and resurrection. But who's counting at harvest time?

You can also draw on the power of the air. Ring bells—church bells are loudest—to silence thunder. Mix in the power of water by sprinkling the bells with holy water, and their sound will push hail back into the clouds. If all you have is your own voice, invoke the power of the angels. Don't stop at the "good" angels like Gabriel or Michael. Panchihel and his forty-four thousand angel helpers would be a good start.

So indeed, when dark clouds appear on the horizon, just smile contentedly. The Middle Ages had weather-wizards, and you're one of them.

HOW *to* SURVIVE
in ENDLESS WINTER

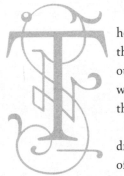

The winter of 1510–1511 was brutal. Harsher than any in recent memory, and (as it turned out) worse than any the inhabitants of Brussels would later see. So, in January, they did the only thing they could: they built snowmen.

Specifically, they built more than one hundred of them, all over the city. Saints made out of snow, Greek gods made out of snow, cows made out of snow. The snowman art gallery even inspired the city's official poet to write about it, and to bring the snowbeings to literary life. For example, the poem's snowcow poops and farts. Because Middle Ages.

A snownun frozen in the act of seduction was funny, and the snowman defecating in the snow castle of one of Brussels's enemies was even funnier. But the 1511 snowman festival was more than a morale boost. In calling their collective creation a wonder, not a miracle, the citizens of Brussels emphasized that people had done it—not God. Snow sculptures of naked people having sex represented the human triumph over winter. Bring on the cold and the dark, snowmen said. Winter will never win.

That's exactly the kind of spunk you'll need to face a winter that's going to last forever.

❧ HOW TO ADAPT

The medieval Sámi (you probably know their modern descendants as the Indigenous people of Norway, Sweden, Finland, and northwest Russia) thrived quite well in a place that was entirely winter, thank you very much. They founded settlements that they lived in every winter and only during winters. Even those silly Vikings needed summer. January and February were the times when the Norse *depended* on the Sámi goods they received from trade or from the forced taxes of early colonialism.

Oh, don't forget—the medieval Sámi could also deal with places that were summer whenever they were there. And by the late Middle Ages, the Sámi groups along the coastlines had taken up new activities (managed fishing!) that made it easier to stay in one place year-round. The Sámi in interior Scandinavia were still the masters of both eternal summer and eternal winter.

In short, the Sámi were ready for anything.

✿ How to Enjoy

So, the Alps in winter.

You've got a choice. Will you pound nails into the bottoms of your boots and your mare's horseshoes? Or will you make like the locals told tourists they did: put a log in the middle of the downhill road, straddle the log and sit, and have someone give you a solid push-off?

Indeed, medieval Europeans knew how to put the wonder in winter wonderland. And the Brussels Museum of Snowmen was just the beginning. Snowball fights in fifteenth-century Germany were apparently so common that priests classified them as a sin. Or perhaps the real problem was that *priests* were getting smacked in the face with snowballs.

Southern writers seem almost jealous of the Sámi, who strapped skis to their feet, reins to their reindeer, and then enjoyed a little frozen-water skiing. Ice skating, on the other hand, could have been the national sport of the medieval Netherlands if the Netherlands had been a nation at the time. An ice-skating accident even set Lidwina of Schiedam on her journey to sainthood, so don't worry if you're a little unsteady at first!

Save up that worry for high medieval Iceland and Scandinavia. Game rules aren't entirely clear, but most of them involved two teams throwing a ball and chasing each other, with full-body contact. If winter weather got even worse than normal, players sometimes moved their games indoors. They used balls that were weighted to hold up against winter winds, so if you have to play in the hall instead of on a field, be careful about the furniture—especially if it belongs to the queen. Oops. You might have bigger problems, though. The thirteenth-century readers of *Egil's Saga* thought it was perfectly realistic for rival teams to start a fight that ended with a player getting an axe in the head.

One hopes that this particular tale grew in the telling.

✺ HOW TO PROFIT

Let the peasants have their balls and axes. If you're a ruling lord or lady, eternal winter is your chance to come out even further ahead in two key areas.

First, money. The Great Famine of 1315 to 1322 resulted from years of bad harvests in France and the Holy Roman Empire. Peasant families watched in agony as their children starved to death. Nobles watched grouchily as household after household defaulted on their taxes of wheat and barley in order to eat whatever scraps might help them survive. But don't worry. The nobility came up with a great new strategy to handle multiple years of bad weather conditions: make farmers pay their tax or rent with money, not crops.

Where the peasants were supposed to *get* that money if they didn't have crops to sell elsewhere . . . well, that was their problem, wasn't it?

Second, status. Fur is the obvious solution to the problem of staying warm, even if it's a little bit expensive. So why don't you—or parliament, or the city council—pass laws regulating who can and can't wear it? In the late Middle Ages, the sumptuary laws that regulated what social groups could and couldn't wear what clothing made a big deal out of fur—fur itself, different kinds of fur, different places on your clothing to use fur.

The worse winter gets, the more everyone is going to want fur. There's no better way to assert your superiority than to control who can wear it. If you handle things right, that "who" can become nobody but you.

✿ How to Adapt, Enjoy, and Profit

There was one unmistakable advantage to winter for western European peasants in the early Middle Ages: less war. So much less. Kings and lords didn't campaign with armies they couldn't maintain, so no one got drafted to fight, and troops weren't ravaging farmers' fields, burning their houses, and worse. Vikings headed home from their summer raiding season. Even the Mediterranean coast, hardly known for brutal winters, got a break—the sea itself was much more dangerous during winter, so shoreline raids by pirates dropped off considerably then.

Well . . . Vikings changed all that. By the mid-ninth century, they'd perfected the art of overwintering: setting up hibernal shop on the islands and river deltas that ringed Europe—Ireland, France, Iberia, *southern* France, you name it. They adapted their life patterns to the new location, enjoyed being somewhat less cold, and profited *majestically* from being able to plunder booty and enslave victims all year round.

Your minor problem here is that the Vikings eventually realized it was better for them all to stop being Vikings per se and just be the ordinary Norse. Their overwinter raiding strategy (not to mention the entire "Viking" business) was good for *a* winter, maybe for *some* winters. But it's not going to be your best bet for eternal winter.

✿ How to Win

In the end, though, there's one group of people in the Middle Ages who knew how to do winter right: monks and nuns. Medieval cloisters set their daily schedules according to sunrise, noon, and sunset. So the monastic day started with a communal prayer at dawn.

In other words, since the winter sun rises later, my friend, you'll get to sleep in. Every day.

119

HOW *to* DEFEAT
the BARBARIAN HORDES

et's be clear about one thing before we even start. In the world surrounding the medieval Mediterranean, everyone was someone else's barbarian horde. For the first 580 years of Islam, for example, Arab writers had some nice things to say about Byzantium itself. It was *al-Rum*, the continuation of ancient Rome's culture and majesty. But the Greeks as a people were either fierce and treacherous men or lustful and seductive women. (You were expecting something different?)

Then the Crusades happened.

In 1098, western Christians invaded the Near East, and in 1099, they slaughtered the residents of Jerusalem. Suddenly Arab writers had much nicer things to say about the Byzantine Christians. Funny how that works.

Let's be clear about another thing. No matter who you were, Vikings were never the good guys. Now please don't tar and feather the Norse overall as "just" Vikings (even if one of their chief exports was tar). The *vikingr* were a small subset of the Norse during a small subset of the Middle Ages who pirated and raided and burned and murdered and enslaved various peoples—including each other. Sure, the medieval horror of and modern romance with the *vikingr* has marked the period of 800 to 1050 as the "Viking Age." It didn't last longer because Vikings, as such, did not last longer. But southern Scandinavia and Iceland stubbornly insisted on remaining populated.

Besides, barbarian hordes never have culture beyond being tough and seemingly evil yet admirable—and the Norse had plenty of culture! True, *Bandamanna Saga* is not as catchy a book title as *Canterbury Tales* or *Inferno* or *Anwar 'ulwiyy al-ajram fi al-kashf 'an asrar al-ahram*. But the Norse sagas are culturally important enough to give us the word "saga" in the first place, and good enough literature to earn it.

Medieval Scandinavia also produced some excellent art. The interlaced scrollwork and stylized animals more usually called Celtic knotwork are best known from the Irish *Book of Kells* (early ninth century) and English *Lindisfarne Gospels* (c. 720). Similar Scandinavian art, however, shows how much they valued the artistic. Oh, you say that Vikings raided and destroyed Lindisfarne Priory in 793, seventy years after the beautiful *Gospels*? Nobody's perfect.

Hmm, and come to think of it, the Norse didn't really get much better after the Viking Age ended. In the high Middle Ages, some Norse lords gradually forced the Sámi people to their north to pay them . . . let's call it "protection money."

So . . . let's just stick with "Vikings were never the good guys."

This is the story of how that worked out for the Vikings, and why it will work out for you.

🌸

Because events in medieval Europe only really matter when they affect England or France, the Viking Age began in 793, when *vikingr* ravaged the English coast just southeast of Edinburgh to a significant extent for the first time. But the various Scandinavian collectives weren't messing around. By 820, raiding parties were well into France and pushing down the Seine River toward Paris. By 840, they had made it to Iberia. The terror of writers in France, Christian Spain, and al-Andalus was justified. (By 842, Viking groups were also *losing* in Iberia, but let's set that aside. Barbarian hordes aren't supposed to lose until they lose to you.)

By 900 or so, Norse groups from Norway and Denmark had plundered large swathes of England and France into submission. And suddenly the question became "Who had had enough?" Because in 911 or so, an otherwise-unknown Viking leader named Rollo (c. 860–930) decided to make a deal with Carolingian emperor Charles the Not-Devious (no, really). The treaty apparently gave Rollo . . . the land he already controlled in exchange for defending it against other attackers.

Subsequent treaties between Rollo's descendants and Charles's successors expanded the Vikings' political control of territory through political means. Part of the deal was even converting to Christianity. Vikings were infamous above all for burning and looting churches and monasteries (possibly because monks and nuns were the ones writing the records), yet Rollo *donated* money and land to the Church.

It's not that the Vikings in Normandy became *French*. (Insofar as you could consider anything in the year 911 to really be "French.") They imposed some Scandinavian laws on their new subjects, and Norse words filtered into the local vocabulary. So the Norman Vikings were still *Vikings*. They took, and they took, and they took. Just . . . they began to prefer doing it through politics and intermarriage, and they began to give as well as take. In short, they were Vikings—but they were no longer *vikingr*. The barbarian hordes were neither barbarians nor hordes.

So Rollo-ver in your Viking-style burial barrow, Erik the Red. King Charles treated western Europe's fiercest foes as equals, showed favor to the wrong nobles, died in prison, and was memorialized as Charles the Not-Devious. But you have to admit that giving the barbarian hordes land that you don't even control and convincing them to adopt your religion is an unorthodox strategy for defeating them.

HOW *to* OUTWIT *a* GENIE

o, you're broke.

Traveling was one of the most expensive things you could do in the Middle Ages (besides spending one-third of France's gross national product to ransom the king in 1250). You've been traveling for a long time now, so you're broke.

You've already grudgingly admitted that heroes don't steal money for personal benefit. For some reason, too, heroes never take a week or two out of their quest to perform a little bit of honest harvest-season labor as a farmhand. That makes you prime genie-bait.

You know how this story goes. You find a lamp; the lamp is inhabited; the lamp's ghostly resident offers to grant you any three wishes in the world; the specter finds a way to twist your requests until you end up rich but dead. Unless, of course, you can find a way to make this genie give you what you thought you were asking for.

The Middle Ages *should* be able to help. Jinn are time-honored spirits of Near Eastern folklore. But the footnote for the familiar wish-granting, lamp-dwelling *jinni*—and successfully deputizing its powers—cites the story "Ala al-Din, or, the Wonderful Lamp," one of the (far fewer than 1,001) stories in *1001 Nights*. The various stories in the *1001 Nights* anthology have roots in cultures stretching back to ancient India, but the large majority of the book is a creation of the early medieval Arabic world.

. . . Except for "Ala al-Din," a story that doesn't show up in copies of *1001 Nights* until 1700s France. Now, 1700s France was many things, such as short on bread and dangerous for heads, but it was definitely not medieval.

So if you want to outwit *your* genie, and keep all the money without losing your life, you'll need to find your strategies somewhere besides actual medieval stories about jinn.

☬ THE NEED TO SEEK GUIDANCE ELSEWHERE WILL BENEFIT YOU

Consider the genuinely medieval *1001 Nights* story "Abu Muhammad hight Lazybones." Abu Muhammad was a man whose preferred lifestyle earned him the nickname "Lazybones." Here's how lazy: when he needed money, he gave what he had to another man to go find something that would make Lazybones a solid profit. The other man's acquisition was unsurprisingly a jinni in disguise. And in fact, Lazybones *did* harness the power of the jinni, and the jinni *did* make him as rich as the caliph.

Of course, in between asking someone else to do the work to make him rich and actually being rich, the man nicknamed Lazybones had to travel through a desert, kill a brown snake to rescue a white snake, travel to space, fall into the ocean, sail almost to China, visit a mythical city, acquire a magical sword, sneak into the city, climb a pillar, and sprinkle musk on a vulture. Also, he had to make friends with several members of the white snake's family, and then harness the power of a whole army of jinn. One might rather imagine that the original jinni outwitted no-longer-Lazybones, even if the human ostensibly won.

You've already got a dragon to slay and a princess who may or may not let you save her. You don't have time to star in what was ultimately a religious morality tale about the value of hard work, too.

☬ STRATEGY #1: BYPASS THE GENIE

You don't have to outwit something you don't deal with in the first place. So when you find the lamp, just melt it down and sell the gold.

On the other hand, what self-respecting genie ever lived in a *big* lamp? If you use this strategy, you'll be alive, but you won't be rich for long.

☫ STRATEGY #2: PROTECT YOURSELF

When you prepare to negotiate with your genie, first draw a magic circle around yourself and recite incantations to cast a spell of protection from the genie's wiles.

On the other hand, what self-respecting genie wouldn't point out that your circle is actually lopsided? And who ever heard of a magic oval?

☫ STRATEGY #3: STOP AFTER TWO WISHES

Genies only start twisting your words after you've made all three wishes, right? So all you have to do is narrow your list down to two, and make sure you never again say something like, "Ugh, I wish they would stop."

On the other hand, you're traveling with a *bard*. You *will*, at some point, wish they would stop.

Just imagine how a self-respecting genie would twist *that* request.

☫ STRATEGY #4: BEAT THE GENIE AT ITS OWN GAME

Writing down your deal with the genie sounds like the worst idea possible. You don't want a record for the genie to consult when determining the best way to twist your words. And yet, putting your wishes in writing is— finally—a foolproof way to prevent the genie from twisting your words. With proper medieval guidance, you can draw up a contract whose words the genie will twist, as a genie does. Just, with the help of the Empress of Hell, they won't be your words.

Oh, right. This is a good time to mention that in medieval Christianity, the mild, loving Mother of God is also a sword-swinging demon slayer.

And I don't mean just metaphorically, by bringing into this world the Son of God who would die on a cross, descend into hell, defeat death, and

125

resurrect himself. No, I mean with an actual sword and actual demons. It was the stuff of books, plays, and stained glass windows—the comic books of the Middle Ages.

For your goal of outwitting a genie, you'll want to turn to Mary's rescue of Theophilus. The legend of the beleaguered Anatolian bishop has taken many forms over the millennium and a half since its apparent origins in . . . Anatolia, so we'll just use the version most popular in the Middle Ages.

Theophilus was a bishop or other Church official who suddenly found himself summarily dismissed from his office—thus, from his influence and his *income*. The wisdom of his subsequent actions suggests the dismissal was not entirely unfounded. To regain his power and his wealth, Theophilus summoned a demon and sold the only thing he had left: his soul.

The devil was crafty. He made sure Theophilus signed, sealed, and gave him a charter that promised Theophilus's soul after death in exchange for riches during life. The devil slid back down the muddy slide to hell with the physical document.

The story then splits briefly into two versions. If priests are telling the story, Theophilus immediately fell into spiritual despair. If nonpriests are telling it, Theophilus rose uncommonly fast through the ranks of the Church and acquired (and spent) the money to match, *then* fell into spiritual despair.

He mustered up the energy to pray to Mary for help, since she was the ultimate intercessor between God and sinful humans. (Essentially, a superpowered saint.) And Mary, the Mother of God and the mother of mercy, naturally took the self-damned man's side. She recognized that the materiality of Theophilus's charter set the terms. To put it simply, Theophilus's soul had become a physical object in a physical location, guarded by a physical entity.

So Mary—not her savior son, but Mary herself—descended to the physical location of hell, fought the devil in single combat, and stole back the charter. Theophilus's soul was saved, and the Queen of Heaven earned her *excellent* late medieval title of Empress of Hell.

126

When priests told the story, the point was a prim lesson about the power of Mary as "mediatrix" and how you should turn to God in times of despair. When nonpriests told the story, the point was that Mary—the Queen of Heaven, the mother of mildness and mercy—grabbed a sword, descended to hell, stole back Theophilus's charter, and then beat up the devil. (Again: stained glass windows, the comic books of the Middle Ages.)

By turning your wishes into a written contract, therefore, you essentially trap their power within a small, delineated space. You shift the means of outwitting away from twisting words to the arena of physical strength. You'll still have to fight the genie for possession of the document. But you're a hero with a sword. Fighting a literal battle instead of a battle over the literal is *your* territory, not some ephemeral spirit's. Even if you don't have the Empress of Hell on your side.

☙ STRATEGY #5: MAKE SURE YOU HAVE A PLAN B

The best part about using the written charter strategy is that unlike basically everything else heroes must do to succeed in their quest, it has its own, nearly built-in fallback strategy.

The devil taught you how to read, sure, but his instruction was only necessary because literacy rates among medieval peasants very nearly did not exist. But by the late Middle Ages, bureaucratic documentation was widespread, and peasants had plenty of occasion to sign various things their landlords and lords presented. Instead of signing their names, illiterate people would substitute an *X*.

So when you draw up that charter with the genie, make sure you hire a scribe to write it, and make sure you hearken back to the days of your prediabolical-literacy youth. You sign your "name" as a big, bold *X*. An *X* that could have been written by anyone.

Now you don't even have to wish that nobody will recognize your handwriting.

Because that kind of wish could go very, very wrong.

HOW *to* FIND *a* UNICORN

here comes a point in every hero's quest when most hope seems lost.

Not *all* hope. That part always comes later, and it's going to require a lot more than an injection of good fortune. But if you *are* losing hope, and are looking for a little bit of good fortune—might I interest you in a slight detour to seek a unicorn?

Let's get one thing out of the way immediately. Medieval Christian theologians were very clear that the unicorn is so powerful and wild, you don't find it—it finds you. Specifically, it walks up to a virgin and rests its head in their lap.

But you and your party don't have time to sit around waiting for a unicorn, or to set a trap so you can mock the village bully for lying about his sexual exploits. And you don't have the villainy to follow through on the next part of the theologians' legend—namely, the part where the gentle unicorn falls asleep in the virgin's lap, and the virgin leads the tame, snuggling unicorn to the nearest castle to be slaughtered.

Really, it's best for everyone if you find the unicorn instead.

You'll need to keep in mind three principles on your happy-ending unicorn hunt.

1. KNOW WHAT YOU'RE LOOKING FOR

"Uni-cornus" is the semirecognizable Latin term for "one horn." And indeed, Latin, Arabic, and Hebrew texts about unicorns describe an animal with one horn that tapers up to a point. From there, though . . .

Natural philosophers in western Europe envisioned unicorns with the body of a goat. (It's the beards.) Some Near Eastern writers described the unicorn as a prematurely born camel, the horn being the result of its mother giving birth before the fetus had solidified. (It's medieval science— just go with it.) One Hebrew pamphlet mentioned a bull-like animal with a horn on its chin and on its nose. (It's sort of like a beard, just without the rest of the goat.)

So much for zoological theory. You need someone who saw a unicorn for himself. You need Marco Polo.

Polo, who was indeed a real person and most likely really took the journey he and his ghostwriter Rusticello claimed, made it from Italy to (among other places) the island of Sumatra and back home again. On Sumatra he saw his unicorn. And thought it was disgusting.

According to Polo and Rusticello, the unicorn is almost the size of an elephant, as ugly as a water buffalo, has a short and thick horn, and likes nothing more than wallowing in swamp and mud. But that sounds like a . . .

Rhinoceros. He's describing a rhinoceros.

Or, one might say—and medieval writers did say—he is describing a rhinoceros, also known as a monoceros. Which is *Greek* for one-horn. Well, then.

The good news is that Bertrandon's worldbuilding of Syrian and Armenian goats is as extraneous as you thought. The bad news is that if you throw out Polo's testimony, you're going to need some different evidence to be sure that unicorns exist for you to find.

❧ 2. DON'T BE FOOLED BY IMITATIONS

Unicorn horn was the hottest of commodities in late medieval Europe thanks to its rumored magical and medicinal properties. Perhaps they were more than rumored. Consider this: Lorenzo de Medici (1449–1492) was willing to cough up six thousand florins if it meant he got a unicorn horn.

129

His brother was not. His brother was also assassinated at the age of twenty-four by people targeting Lorenzo. Lorenzo died peacefully in his bed. European monarchs, meanwhile, had enough experience to trust unicorn horns with a much more specific task. When powdered and mixed into a drink, horn could neutralize any assassin's poison.

Thus, since unicorns as such did not actually exist in the Middle Ages but medieval people believed they owned real unicorn horns, you'll have to be on your guard against . . . being fooled by the same imitators.

Okay, fine, powdered unicorn horn is easy enough to avoid because its chances of not being ground-up rock are essentially zero. In fact, because you're the hero, the hordes of evil are actively trying to kill you, so the percentage chance of the powder being the poison instead of the antidote is one hundred.

But Lorenzo owned *something* that had to look like a unicorn horn. If you're a Thule expert whaler from Greenland, you already know exactly what: a narwhal tusk.

Technically a narwhal tooth (really), these tusks are long, thin, taper to a point, and are spiraled like a helix. In other words, exactly how western European artists depicted the horns atop unicorns' heads. And if you're a Thule hunter, you could do quite well for yourself trading narwhal tusks to Norse traders.

If you're not a Thule hunter, you should just keep in mind that somewhere between Baffin Bay and Lorenzo's Florence, someone bought a narwhal tusk and sold a unicorn horn.

(No, you can't be that someone.)

♛ 3. LOOK IN THE RIGHT PLACES

On the other hand, unicorn horn–owning Lorenzo de Medici did survive an assassination attempt while his tightfisted brother died. Even if it's essentially the magical version of the placebo effect, perhaps narwhals and rhinos are close enough to unicorns to count.

There's still one problem: good luck approaching them safely. Especially the part where you swim in the Arctic to get to said narwhal.

So after crossing Greenland and Sumatra off your list of nonviolent hunting grounds, it's time to look to the other edges of the world. Specifically, to the royal court of Ming-era China after 1414, when the sultan of Bengal gave the emperor a giraffe.

Bengal—the future northeastern India and western Bangladesh—was not exactly known for its expansive African savannas. But its sultan had gone to great literal lengths (possibly to a royal menagerie in Arabia; more likely to one of the Swahili city-states in southeastern Africa) to obtain such a special diplomatic gift for China.

The enthusiastic Chinese reception justified Bengal's effort. The giraffe was still showing up in luxury art a century later, and multiple nobles *wrote poetry* about it. To find out why it was such a prize, you'll want to page through the *Ming Shi-lu*, essentially a galactic-scale scrapbook compiled over nearly three centuries of medieval and early modern Chinese history. The giraffe receives only a prim mention as part of a list of other 1414 Bengalese gifts: horses, beautiful fabrics, local delicacies. Except the imperial bureaucrat doesn't say *zulafa* (the Chinese equivalent of Arabic's *zurafa*—giraffe). He writes *qi-lin*.

A qi-lin is a mythical animal associated with good fortune in Chinese folklore. (Sound familiar?) Descriptions vary (sound familiar?), but might include the body of a deer, the feet of a horse, the tail of a cow, the scales of a fish . . . oh, and one horn.

True, qi-lin is not *literally* "one horned" in the sense of uni-cornus. From ancient Chinese poetry, the name seems to have the meaningful etymology of "a female lin." But description-wise, it's a whole lot closer to a unicorn than the rhino.

The first lesson here is to feel sympathy for the poor, misunderstood rhino. (Sympathy from a safe distance, mind you.) The second lesson is the recognition that the Chinese saw a new-to-them animal and translated it **131** into a unicorn.

Were they convinced the giraffe was a true qi-lin? Or were they trying to make sense of a foreign animal they didn't recognize?

In the end, it doesn't really matter. (More to the point: the sources don't tell you.) You're looking for good fortune and a good distraction. And you know perfectly well that there are few things better than a *giraffe* in *medieval China*.

WHERE *to* DIG
for BURIED TREASURE

ugsburg, May 1544. The tall woman drew a circle in the dirt with a sword as a priest read out loud from a book and swung a censer. Regina Koch, the owner of the house and yard, who knew full well what was happening, watched from inside with a friend. The woman walked around the circle bearing a candle and sprinkling holy water onto the ground. She walked over to a different spot and scratched lines in the earth with her sword, then sat down next to it.

The woman read out loud from her own little book, made the sign of the cross repeatedly, then turned to the group of men standing behind her and told them it was time. They recited several Bible verses—and started digging.

Some context. Augsburg, May 1544: Split between Catholics and Protestants, Augsburg seethed with religious fervor like few other places. Just ahead loomed one of the city's fiercest witch panics, which ended with 150 people executed. When Koch and her co-conspirators were betrayed to civic authorities by a nosy neighbor, what terrible fate could await them?

The unknown woman was named as Sophia Voit of Nuremberg and sent home, Koch was sent to jail but pardoned, and the diggers were ordered to confine themselves for four to eight days. The judges could condemn the events as superstitious and demonic all they wanted, but the punishments told a very different tale.

Throughout the medieval world, the idea of buried treasure lived in the twilight lands between religion and magic, science and ritual, hopeful dreams and devoured souls. And, of course, between mystical lore and straight-up greed. In other words, exactly the kind of thing that made you want to be a hero in the first place.

The lure of treasure knows no boundaries, even for heroes who would *never* mess with straight-up greed, including you. *Never.* Bourgeois widow Regina Koch, who was nothing at all like you, let magicians dig in her backyard, the party swearing to split any discoveries. A voyager all the way from India supposedly delved into the Great Pyramid in search of riches he never found. (This voyager was also nothing at all like you, especially because he was probably not a real person.) Desperate impoverished men (real men) begged wealthy Cairenes to fund their expeditions.

Scholars safely ensconced in monasteries and madrasas couldn't resist, either. Jewish writers from Iberia to Egypt copied treasure-hunting manuals from Arabic letters into Hebrew ones. (Did I mention there were treasure-hunting manuals?) English priest Robert of Ketton (c. 1110–1160) translated multiple astrological treasure-hunting manuals (see?) into Latin. Then there were the Egyptian nobles who hired illiterate day laborers to do their pyramid-plundering for them.

Did I mention that treasure-hunting became an organized profession in medieval Egypt?

The concept of government-sanctioned grave desecration, already popular in later ancient Egyptian dynasties, gained new life in the Middle Ages. Tenth-century leaders turned it into a guild of sorts called "the seekers," and by "a guild of sorts" I mean "so the government could tax the profits."

For medieval seekers, ancient buried treasure was certainly not limited to gold. Long-plundered tombs—for those who dared disturb the dead—could yield profits with scrapings of mummies; European Christians were as wild for *mummia* as they were for the spices of the Far East. Books of ancient magic, on the other hand, could point the way to exponentially more treasure hoards.

Nor was ancient buried treasured limited to, well, being ancient or buried. The Egyptian elite of all religions lavished each other with sparkling gifts and displayed even more in their homes. It didn't take much for people to start whispering about the origins of such stunning wealth.

Treasure-hunting in the Middle Ages nevertheless had a low success rate and a high death rate. Even for those who scoffed at demons, there might be traps made by very human hands. Baghdadi skeptic Abu Bakr al-Jassas told the story of a temple and tomb guarded first by a staircase. To climb it would trigger, through a series of levers, hidden blades that whipped out at the unfortunate seeker and beheaded him.

So, when it's time to find the buried treasure, choose wisely among the available astrological calculations or magical amulets. You can go the quick (and pious!) route to cross potentially cursed water, as Ibn Al-Haj Al-Tilmsani al-Maghrabi suggests. Write out a specific verse from the Qur'an into a magic table, one word in each of its squares: "Say, 'Just think: if all your water were to sink deep into the earth, who could give you flowing water in its place?'"[9]

Or, if you're *really* committed, follow one of al-Maghrabi's other suggestions: After praying for forty-seven days and dealing with a ghost accompanied by a lion, a human ghost with a dog's head, and seventy ghosts wearing green, you will see a white city shining on a hilltop. You must then go to the green silk tent at the castle gates and find the golden throne inside.

At that point, a man named al-Taous will appear, with seventy men dressed in white beside him, and both good and evil jinn above him. Offer him incense, which he will burn, and the men dressed in white will eat. Finally, you can ask al-Taous for the secret knowledge you seek. Be sure to use the precise words: "O King al-Taous, I request from you the secret of turning rocks and opening caves and homes and whatever more I want."[10]

From that moment on, the king will order his good and evil jinn to open anything you want any time you read the spell, as long as there is

9   Q67:30, trans. M.A.S. Abdel Haleem's translation from the Oxford World's Classics edition.
10   Okasha El Daly, *Egyptology: The Missing Millennium: Ancient Egypt in Medieval Arabic Writings* (UCL Press, 2005), 36–37.

incense burning to feed them. The hidden things of the world are yours to possess. Only one question remains: *At what cost?*

Spirits and demons, insisted the wisest medieval scholars, could never be bound by mere human words. Demons permitted spells to give people the temporary illusion of power. The true result was to bind would-be witches to their will. Just ask the tall woman from Nuremberg who stepped into the circle in Regina Koch's yard. Almost two hundred years earlier, a Spanish priest offered his own ritual that made no effort to disguise who was truly in control: "Let them show honor or veneration or worship of the invoked demons by drawing a circle in the earth; placing a boy in the circle; with a mirror, sword, vessel, or other small body set up near the boy, with the necromancer holding the book, and reading, and calling upon the demon."[11]

The German sorcerers who drew the magic circle and read aloud the necromantic words thought they were gaining the supernatural power to find treasure. The Spanish priest admits outright that the spellcaster is worshipping demons.

So after—I mean before you start digging for treasure, ask yourself: What *did* happen that day in Regina Koch's backyard? And are you really ready to find out?

---

11 Michael Bailey, "From Sorcery to Witchcraft: Clerical Conceptions of Magic in the Later Middle Ages," *Speculum* 76, no. 4 (2001): 972. I discuss the parallel in Cait Stevenson, "The Necromancer, the Inquisitor, and the Hunt for Buried Treasure in the Late Middle Ages," *Medieval Studies Research Blog*, University of Notre Dame, October 16, 2020, https://sites.nd.edu/manuscript-studies/2020/10/16/the-necromancer-the-inquisitor-and-the-hunt-for-buried-treasure-in-the-late-middle-ages/.

HOW *to* FIGHT *the* FIRE

64 CE: An old woman supposedly dropped a candle . . . and definitely burned down giant swathes of Constantinople. 532: A chariot race set off riots . . . that burned down large swathes of Constantinople. Again. 1203 and 1204: A series of fires burned down less than one-third of Constantinople, but essentially allowed the Latin invaders to conquer the whole city.

Fire itself was beyond necessary, of course. In the Middle Ages, using open flame was not optional. But if just one English chicken kicked over a candle onto a perfectly average straw floor, it was going to be a hot time in the very old town that night.

Unless medieval people got in the way.

Which they did. And which you will, too.

Fortunately, the firefighting instructions they left behind might seem rather familiar.

❧ 1. CURFEW

Forget the cold. Ever get annoyed at night when you have to turn out the light and go to bed? Holy woman Agnes Blannbekin (d. 1316) sure did. But she dutifully obeyed Vienna's literal curfew—medieval French and English *cuevre-feu*, the hour you had to "cover fire" at night. Can't leave open flame unattended.

❧ 2. ZONING LAWS

A blacksmith's workshop next to where a carpenter sells wooden furniture: not so good. City street names tell how once upon a time, artisans grouped near other people in their craft. Islamic theologians very much wanted these districts to be the law, but theologians weren't running cities. Some crafts were better than others at sticking together, but most people ended up rezoning themselves into rich and poor neighborhoods. Thus, by 1500 you had streets like Augsburg's Baker Lane, where one in three buildings either made or sold beer instead.

⚜ 3. BUILDING CODES

"The whole street is on fire!" you hear, and probably picture a row of burning buildings. Nope. In medieval Europe, it could mean the very literal street was on fire, especially if the town had used wooden slats to pave its roads. One Norwegian city learned this lesson the hard way in 1476 and started paving its wooden streets with gravel. To deal with interior threats, Damascus wanted buildings to have stone chimneys. The city was even willing to pay to enclose and cover its main market with stone.

Meanwhile, many Europeans made their roofs out of thatch, which is famous for never catching fire.

⚜ 4. FIRE EXTINGUISHERS

Basically, everywhere in the Middle Ages demanded that people keep a bucket of water by the door at all times. Blacksmiths' shops were more likely to start fires and carpenters' shops were more likely to catch fire, so Cairo mandated in 1321 that those shopkeepers keep *two* buckets.

When the buckets ran out, desperate residents turned to prayer. Greek Christians in Constantinople's massive 464 fire begged divine forgiveness for neglecting their patron saint. Cairo's citizens fled to mosques, climbed minarets, and cried out for divine aid.

⚜ 5. CONTAINMENT

One house on fire was probably a goner, but you might have time to protect the ones next door. People in late medieval Nuremberg climbed ladders to throw buckets of water onto those buildings' upper stories as well as the ground level. But that was a best-case scenario. More often, people in places like Damascus tried to dismantle reed roofs, and everyone from England to Ethiopia sometimes just tore down entire houses—no matter that many houses were built to be strong enough to stand for hundreds of years.

🌾 6. FIREFIGHTERS

A fire in a medieval city all too quickly became an entire medieval city on fire. Throughout most of the Middle Ages and most of the medieval world, firefighter recruitment meant an on-the-spot decision between "I don't want my house to burn down today" and "Maybe I should just grab my stuff and run today." (Baghdadi scholars saved their library in 1117: the real heroes.)

Cities in Syria and Italy had self-organized groups (gangs?) of younger men who might mobilize to fight a fire in any part of their city. Or they might get blamed for starting it. Were they teenage rebels, or militias with hard-core political beliefs? Later writers sure had opinions.

By the 1400s, German cities had made major improvements. Nuremberg subdivided its eight quarters (. . . the city had grown) into units for firefighting and defense, and local captains assigned every able-bodied man a particular role in confronting fire. The city offered rewards to the people and units who showed up first, which is probably why the system worked.

🌾 7. WATER

Medieval hydraulics were . . . actually pretty great. Germany's mountain-top castles with no access to flowing water dug impossibly deep wells and developed rudimentary filtration for their underground reservoirs. The cities of hilly Italy learned to dig horizontally into the surrounding hillsides, in order to access underground aquifers without needing to pump anything uphill.

Expanding cities meant the water had to reach a bigger area, and tax-funded pipeworks were a great way to do it. The oldest cities in Europe may even have inherited functional pipe systems from Roman days. Meanwhile,

Muslim engineers in Yemen, Syria, and Spain were busy inventing new irrigation systems that cities used for their water supply, too. People still liked their private wells, but by the 1200s, no modern town wanted to be without its own lead, clay, or wooden pipes.

♛ 8. FIRE HYDRANTS

The saying "beggars can't be choosers" was all too literal for the lower-class workers paid to take rich men's spots in the fire brigades of Nuremberg. This phrase also applied to their water sources. Public bathhouses were required to supply water (how's that for spa service?); wells were useful but slow. The cities of Freiburg im Breisgau and Zurich especially encouraged the reuse of dirty water for firefighting.

But best of all were the fountains.

True, "fountain" in medieval sources might just mean a pipe that emptied into some kind of channel. And those fountains were just as useful—and used—as bigger ones when it came to firefighting. But the city of Siena would not have thrown a massive festival in 1343 for a pipe with a new tank. No, its residents were celebrating the final completion of the city piazza's large, lavish fountain, which for a time was even adorned with an antique statue of Venus. Goslar, in Germany, topped its twelfth-century fountain with a bronze eagle—a Roman and medieval symbol of strength, empire, and renewal. The palace at Aachen had its own gorgeous fountain in the shape of a bronze pine cone. The pine cone was in fact a second Roman and medieval symbol of renewal . . . but you'll notice that emperors always chose a symbolic eagle instead.

♛ 9. FIRE HOSES AND FIRE ENGINES

Whatever your source, there were essentially two ways to get *enough* water from it to the fire. You could put buckets on a cart, or you could carry the buckets yourself. (Remember the part about rich Nurembergers paying poor ones to take their places? Right.)

❧ 10. WATER BALLOONS

Yes, ladders have their place when fighting a fire; yes, buckets are nice and refillable. But wouldn't you rather fill a clay pot with water, hurl it at a burning house, and watch the pot smash to pieces? Yes, yes you would.

❧ AFTERMATH

This pagan symbolism of pine cones was *probably* not on people's minds while they watched an entire city block burn to the ground or tried desperately to keep it from happening. It probably wasn't on their minds the next day, either, as they cried over what they'd lost (everything), gossiped over who had started it (it had to be old women or Jewish people, of course), and grumbled about looting (kids these days).

But then in the 1350s, Nuremberg shoved its Jewish population into a burned-out quarter of the city that no one had dared touch since a 1340 fire. The ultimate result? A thriving neighborhood complete with kosher butchers.

And consider that apple you're holding. There is the small problem about "Eve and Adam eating the apple and unleashing evil into the world," yes. But apples are small and durable, good for travel and better for pies. And if you plucked it from a city orchard, that tree probably grew from the ashes of the house that had once stood in its place. Fires destroyed, but they couldn't defeat.

HOW *to* BRING *the* OLD GODS BACK

he legendary grave robber Ridwan al-Farras knew it as well as you do: the deader the god, the better the god.

The actual existence of any deity, or the correctness of a given religion, is irrelevant here. Contemporary religions are things the people in your village believe. Worse, they are the things your *parents* believe. But heroes fight the mainstream. Heroes are in touch with the secrets of the past. In touch with the outcast gods destroyed by religion and abandoned by their people. In touch with the deepest truths that hold so much more power than (or really, are just plain old cooler than) anything believed in your time. A proper heroic quest awakens the arcane gods and unleashes their power into heroic hands.

That's how the story goes, right?

When al-Farras and his friends passed over the threshold into the cool darkness of the Great Pyramid at Giza, they sure knew it. At least, al-Farras did. As the pyramid stubbornly refused to reveal any gold, his friends gave up and turned back to the mundane world. But not al-Farras. He pressed on alone, his torch flickering against the narrow passageway inside the Great Pyramid. The last his friends heard from him was a terrified scream.

Until he materialized out of the wall, bathed in red.

Crying out at them in a language he did not speak, the language of the pyramid builders, al-Farras warned them to go no farther. All who disturbed the peace of the pyramids would share in his eternal punishment. And he sank slowly into the ground, never to be seen again.

Still sure you want to bring the Old Gods back? Don't say I didn't warn you.

❁ STRATEGY #1: USE THE PYRAMIDS

Had ancient human or supernatural forces built the pyramids? Either way, the Fatimid dynasty was quite eager to take advantage. These powerful Muslim rulers (909–1171) founded their new capital at Cairo, right across the river from Giza and its monuments. They chose to rule from the shadow of the greatest pyramids, with all the magic, treasures, and hidden wisdom from the past. Fatimid caliphs and their heirs brought the Old Gods back to life, but only to embellish their own majesty.

A few individual rulers had more creative definitions of "embellishing the majesty." Abu'l Hasan Mu'nis (d. 933) offered a bounty to the first person who could climb to the top of the Great Pyramid. Two hundred years later, the Fatimid government staged massive nighttime parties around the Giza pyramids. One century after that, al-Malik al-Kamil upstaged them both, as he held climbing contests *and* threw giant parties. Obviously, these rulers understood that poor Ridwan's tale was just part of the never-ending superstition about cursed Egyptian mummies and tombs.

On the other hand, all these caliphs made sure the Nile would always safely separate their palaces from Giza. Throwing parties and hiding behind a river are two good ways to keep the Old Gods very much present but *very* much sleeping.

Rulers from later dynasties would snort at the Fatimid caliphs. You can't bring the Old Gods back, they would say, so stop trying. These leaders thought they could outdo the pyramids in majesty and plundered the pyramids' stones for building projects. The great sultan and general Saladin (1138–1193), who was beloved for his chivalry and charity—even by the Christian crusaders he defeated—ordered the destruction of Giza's smaller pyramids. It was easier and cheaper to use their stones than to carve out his own. And subsequent leaders followed his example. The magnificent stone

143

casings that once dazzled Giza's visitors were dismantled piece by piece, ruler by greedy ruler.

On the other hand, the pyramids held their own against the exterior vandals. Saladin's own son reportedly spent eight months and *12,000 dinars* trying to repeat his father's deed with one of Giza's smaller surviving pyramids. And completely, utterly failed.

Vandalism: not a good way to bring the Old Gods back.

♛ STRATEGY #2: STAY FAR, FAR AWAY FROM THEM

Parties, plunder, treasure hunters looting the insides, and graffiti artists carving on the outside. What more could there possibly be?

Ghost stories. There could be ghost stories. Everyday Cairenes spooked each other with tales of locked chambers guarded by golden idols, of a tomb sealed behind seven gem-encrusted doors, of walls engraved with unreadable words that betrayed all the secrets of the world.

Visiting Jews and Christians borrowed the locals' tradition and added their own legends. *The Travels of John Mandeville* was the best-selling travel guide of medieval Europe, reminding its readers the pyramids were the silos built by biblical hero Joseph. (There is a slight wrinkle in that John Mandeville was probably not a real person and thus he probably never went to Egypt.)

Yet "some men say," whispered the real author, with all the credibility of the supposed knightly narrator, "that [the pyramids] are sepulchres of great lords, who lived sometime." Those tombs, he added, were filled with snakes. And yes, it had to be snakes—how better to enthrall his readers than with tombs of the ancients guarded by the slithering creatures of the devil?

Fan fiction: either a good way to bring the Old Gods back and control them, or a better reason to not even try.

144 ♛ STRATEGY #3: EXPLAIN THE PYRAMIDS

Adventure stories are great, sure. There were also plenty of nonfictional travelers from around the medieval world who made it to Egypt and saw the pyramids for real, and they had just as much to say.

Their writing should have been a good introduction to the twilight world beyond the edges of Islam, Judaism, Christianity, Hinduism, and indigenous Berber beliefs: the realm of inexplicable supernatural powers. Visitors described the pyramids at Giza and Saqqara as unfathomably large, as the greatest marvels in the world. It was obvious that the pyramid builders also made the Sphinx at Giza. Surely it was some kind of idol to hold back the ever-encroaching, ever-consuming desert.

But travel writers inevitably stripped away the mysticism. Most repeated the party line that the pyramids were in fact silos to store grain for famines—silos that were mentioned in the Tanakh, the Bible, and the Qur'an. Muslim travelers insisted that those creepy, unreadable inscriptions on the pyramid exteriors were just using a different alphabet to explain Islam.

Some visitors with a little more education promoted the idea that the pyramids were tombs built for (really) Aristotle and Alexander the Great. Fifteenth-century Italian rabbi Meshullam ben Menahem had the audacity to claim that the pyramids were treasure chambers. He explained this by stating that he could go into Cairo and buy pyramid souvenirs (or counterfeit souvenirs) on the street.

One way or another, visitor after visitor explained away the pyramids. Somehow or other, the mysterious monuments were just regular parts of their historical, religious, *comfortable* world. Old Gods need not apply.

The book called (really) *Lights Lofty of Form in Revealing the Secrets of the Pyramids* should have lived up to its name.[12] Its author, Abu Ja'far al-Idrisi (d. 1251), was unimpressed by the Joseph-grain-famine story. He was also skeptical of the theory that Aristotle ordered the pyramids' construction for Alexander and himself.

Al-Idrisi much preferred a different theory: the pyramids preserved

---

12 The title as translated by Martyn Smith, "Pyramids in the Medieval Islamic Landscape: Perceptions and Narratives," *Journal of the American Research Center in Egypt* 43 (2007): 1.

ancient wisdom to survive catastrophe. Arcane wisdom plus apocalypse already sounds like an idea worthy of "lights lofty of form in revealing secrets." It gets better. The pyramids were built at the command of the ancient Babylonian wise man Hermes Trismegistus, master of all knowledge. What secrets could hieroglyphs hold, besides the wisdom so long lost to the world? And why choose pyramids of stone, unless the builders wanted them to survive even bigger disasters than the Flood that couldn't sink Noah's wooden ark?

Except even *Lights Lofty of Form in Revealing the Secrets* turned out to be less of a crystals-and-cultural-appropriation read, and more theological treatise. Long before al-Idrisi, Muslim theologians had turned the mythical Hermes Trismegistus into an ancestor of Muhammad (under a different name, though) in the Qur'an. He was special, but also just another religious figure. Trismegistus's occult knowledge was astrology and alchemy, which seem plenty mysterious and arcane but were really just two regular medieval sciences. *Lights Lofty* was an impressive and original book, but also just mundane teachings.

Textbooks: a pretty boring way to bring the Old Gods back, even if the title is great.

ꙮ STRATEGY #4: DON'T EXPLAIN THE PYRAMIDS

But there was another theory floating around—one that al-Idrisi tried to cover up and few other people dared mention. This theory agrees with al-Idrisi's belief that the pyramids can and will survive until the apocalypse.

On the other hand, this theory has no use for astrology, alchemy, or Trismegistus under any name. Instead, it whispers that we do not now and never will know the secrets of the pyramid builders. We will never know what they knew. We will never know who they were. For all the splendor of their monuments, the builders have vanished.

146 And herein lies the reason that people in the Middle Ages partied at the pyramids, plundered the pyramids, and explained the existence of the

pyramids as anything except the creation of unknown gods or people. The great monuments had endured to that day. They testified to human expertise, craftsmanship, and glory. They revealed a height of skill that medieval writers had never observed in their own time.

And yet, even the people who built the greatest marvels in the world could vanish without a trace. Those who dared to create monuments meant to last forever had still crumbled to dust. And in their silence, the pyramids proclaimed "You will crumble, too."

WINNING the WAR

HOW *to* LIGHT *the* BEACONS

ith Vikings just off the Scottish coast in the days of Earl Rognvald, the people of Orkney didn't hesitate. The glowing flames on the horizon leapt from island to island, blazing their warning far more quickly than any ship could sail or any pigeon could fly. And the message continued to pass by fire and smoke until all the people were warned.

Oh, indeed, people in the Middle Ages called for aid with signal fires. Wouldn't you? Fire beacons were part of the mythological past that medieval Europe so admired, supposedly used to herald world-shattering events like the fall of Troy. In fact, they were so important in the Middle Ages that Europeans found every way they could to teach heroes just like you (or more realistically, heroes' helpers like your traveling companions) how to light the beacons to warn of approaching doom.

❧ 1. LINGUISTICS (No, REALLY)

Early medieval English kingdoms may not have realized it, but they probably lit their signal fires on the graves of their predecessors. You say long-gone Iron Age people built flat-topped hills called barrows as funerary mounds? And that Saxons also used them as cemeteries in the post-Roman days? Perfect! The seemingly random scattering of place names based on Old English words for "lookout" is not so random if you can arrange them into chains connecting Mercian or

Wessex settlements. It's even less random when experiments show that fire and smoke can actually be seen from one to another.

✿ 2. LAWS

Aragon, Portugal, and all the other kingdoms fighting it out on the Spanish frontier quickly established two cardinal rules of conquest. The best way to claim land was to get people to move there, and the best way to steal it was to kill or enslave them. The people involved in the moving process learned that signal fires were a great way to lower their chances of being involved in the killing and enslavement process. Town laws from the eleventh to the thirteenth century grew increasingly specific about what people were at least *supposed* to do when a riding messenger brought news of a threat to the town or castle.

Are you a town watchman? Great—light a signal fire on top of the watchtower and make sure the church rings its bells. An ordinary villager who sees the fire? If you hurry to the castle gates fast enough, they might even have room for some of your livestock. But the unluckiest had twenty-four hours to get themselves and their weapons to the nearest town or militia, and thus risk of death. Twenty-four hours . . . or sometimes twelve.

So, when someone comes running into your courtyard yelling that the beacons of Aragon are lit, you better grab your sword and *run*.

✿ 3. CHRONICLES

Medieval chronicle writers take pride in recounting their victories over aquatic threat, to . . . varying . . . degrees of trustworthiness. (Pro tip: providing place names tends to make your account a little more reliable.) It's Charlemagne's grandson who casually mentions how his very clever grandpa set up beacons along the Seine River so the warning could beat the boats to Paris. A man who may or may not have been named Ernoul, and who may or may not have seen it for himself, described a true beacon network in Crusader Syria that radiated outward from Damascus until all the land was roused.

Or set chronicles aside and check out Byzantine military manuals. Some of these guides are old-fashioned and theoretical. But some talk about a tenth-century chain of fire stretching hundreds of miles from Constantinople in the north down to the Taurus Mountains near the Syrian border. Archaeologists have evidence that this beacon system actually existed.

4. COMPLAINING

The men who actually had to, you know, *sit on the towers* during English king Edward III's reign (r. 1327–1377) were exactly as thrilled about it as you will be. Letters, regulations, and every other use of writing on parchment flew back and forth trying to make sure the beacons had people to light them.

Okay, fine, you only need four, five, or six people to actually *run* one of the coastal beacons. The response battalions only have to be able to *see* it. Oh, the wood's getting wet? That's no excuse; start using pitch as fuel instead.

No, the Black Death doesn't mean you can stay home. Yes, really, *all* of you are getting drafted. And you have to move to near the coast as long as the French are out there. (No, it doesn't matter that the French navy is terrible.)

But the *real* complaining about the coastal beacon system—the strongest evidence of all for its existence—came from exactly who you'd expect: the people who had to fund it. *All* the people who had to fund it. For instance, there's the don't make us send money, Canterbury edition. Don't make us send money, Devon edition. Don't make us send money, Kent and Sussex and Budleigh and Surrey and *Parliament* edition. Evidently the real problem in England was taxation *with* representation.

※

Of course, even if you weren't one of the people staring at the same stretch of empty ocean all day, every day, beacon systems had their downsides. The authors of the Norse sagas, writing their stories halfway between history and legend, certainly envisioned plenty of them. Their characters crafted or suffered from false alarms triggered by elaborate Viking strategies and false alarms triggered by ordinary fishing boats. Then they had sword fights over who to blame for the false alarms.

Other possible issues: You run out of wood and don't have the time to replace it; you run out of wood and don't have the money to replace it. You don't run out of wood, but an enemy saboteur poured water over all the available wood and it won't burn. One saga author tried to explain away a Viking invasion by insisting that the beacon guardians were so intent on scrutinizing the eastern horizon for fires that they just . . . forgot to look to the west.

And sometimes it was just the universe in general that ruined things. In December 1346, Edward III gave up and sent everyone home because, in short, England has terrible weather.

HOW *to* SAVE *the* PRINCESS

Because actual princesses tend to have their own thoughts on whether or not they need rescuing (and whether or not they want you to do it), you might need a few more people than usual to provide guidance. So, listen up.

We'll ease in slowly with the piece of advice you probably don't need; that the place you wanted to be in the Middle Ages was literally anywhere except the Byzantine court. The place where Princess Euphrosyne, our exemplum, was born? The Byzantine court.

Her mother, Maria, would have made the better fairy-tale princess. Maria was the daughter of a good-hearted but bumbling father from a rural area in the north of Anatolia. In 788, she was (supposedly) chosen for her beauty to journey to the imperial capital at Constantinople and (supposedly) compete for the hand of none other than Emperor Constantine VI.

Constantine had previously been betrothed to the daughter of Charlemagne (yes, that Charlemagne). And yet he (or possibly his mother, Irene) chose the daughter of an unnamed, obscure nobleman from a backwater province instead. The royal couple quickly had two daughters, Euphrosyne and her younger sister, Princess also Irene.

Unfortunately for all involved, Constantine VI was also the emperor who:

- lost a bunch of wars
- had to blind and castrate his rivals to hold
  on to power

- divorced and exiled Maria and his own daughters
- married his mistress
- was blinded and deposed *by his own mother*
- and ended up so hated that nobody even bothered to note what year he died

Byzantine court politics do not mess around.

Thus, Maria's Prince Charming proved to be somewhat less than charming, and in 795 she ended up unhappily exiled to an island monastery along with her kindergarten-age daughters: a true fairy tale ending hardly the happily ever after of a fairy tale. So, enter Maria and Constantine's older daughter, our true heroine: Princess Euphrosyne.

Well, first enter the parts where

- Constantine's mother blinded, deposed, and exiled her own son
- (This is your periodic reminder that anesthesia does not yet exist)
- Nikephoros deposed and exiled then-Empress Irene
- Emperor Nikephoros defeated a coup
- Emperor Nikephoros lost his head in battle one day and ... lost his head
- (On the other hand, sometimes anesthesia isn't very useful)
- Staurakios inherited the throne for two entire months
- Michael I deposed, exiled, and possibly assassinated Emperor Staurakios
- Leo V deposed and exiled Emperor Michael I, eyes and organs intact

155

- To prevent future rebellions, Emperor Leo V castrated Michael I's sons
- (But sometimes you really do want anesthesia)

There was also the part where Leo V decided his *military* expertise qualified him to make a sweeping change to *Christianity itself* that turned a whole bunch of high-ranking Byzantines into heretics overnight. Minor details.

So now it's 820. Now ex-Empress Maria, ex-wife of the emperor *five emperors ago*, is locked behind convent walls and seething. Twenty-five-year-old Princess Euphrosyne has spent nearly her entire life behind those convent walls.

Now the princess is ready to be rescued. Five emperors, one empress, and two attempted emperors later.

👑 THE PRINCE

Because this is ~~the opposite of a real~~ fairy tale, the future Michael II (770–829) probably began life as an uneducated peasant. Even better, he was possibly born into a religious sect scorned by both iconophiles and iconoclasts alike. (A feat that took some effort and did not have good consequences for its believers.)

As the story goes, Michael only joined the Byzantine army because it was a family obligation. He had a speech disability and no formal education, let alone even the most remote of political positions. But none of those stopped him from distinguishing himself for bravery and skill in battle. During the 790s, he rose to military prominence under the watch of the great general Leo.

Naturally, Michael and Leo *did* decide to mess around with Byzantine court politics. Somehow, though, the two of them survived more than a decade of imperial intrigue as close confidants. You can guess how this part of the story goes. In 813, Leo ascended to the throne as Emperor Leo V, secured the line of succession, and elevated Michael to one of the highest-ranking government positions. Michael wasn't ready to rescue anyone just yet. But he was another step closer.

In 820, the warm and fuzzy story of a mentor and his protégé came to the tragic and bloody end you were expecting. Michael had spent some number of years building a military faction behind Leo's back—until the last months of 820, when Leo figured this out and threw him into the sort of jail from which people do not come back out.

And of all people, it was Leo's wife—his dear, dear Theodosia—who may or may not have spearheaded her husband's murder. She convinced Leo to delay Michael's execution, which turned out to be just long enough for Michael's forces to kill the emperor first. In a church. During the service. *On Christmas Day.*

Whether or not Theodosia had organized the Christmas mocking, the imperial crown became Michael's Christmas gift to himself. He thanked Theodosia for her service to the empire by castrating and exiling her and Leo's sons instead of castrating and executing them.

And so, 820 becomes 821. The princess has been ready to be saved for a while now, and now there is a prince mostly charming who can save her.

✻ Nope, Not Quite Yet

Michael's reign was born in tragedy and raised in tears, because this is Byzantium. His *other* friend from his army days had *also* spent Leo's reign gathering a faction of military supporters. But while Michael built his power in Constantinople—the imperial capital, importantly, but still just one city—Thomas did so in all of Anatolia.

And the two of them weren't about to break the chain of emperor bloodshed by making some kind of Christmas treaty. Thomas laid siege to Constantinople. Michael called in the Bulgarians. The Anatolians defeated the Bulgarians in battle. The Bulgarians somehow ended up the real winners. And in 823 Thomas ended up dead.

But things hadn't exactly been better inside besieged Constantinople than outside it, because this is Byzantium. Michael was fifty years old when 157 the imperial crown was placed on his head, so like most Byzantine men that age, he had a wife and child.

In 823, Michael oversaw the execution of his former friend, crawled exhausted into bed—and woke up to the death of his wife.

❦ THE RESCUE

You'll recall that Leo V had turned either himself or the entire Byzantine religious establishment into heretics. Then he had been horrifically murdered in church on a religious holiday. Michael and his allies learned their lesson. They decided to break only small Church rules, in hopes that God wouldn't bother to punish them for such minor sins. Or rather, they wanted someone to break Church rules on their behalf. Because there were three facts:

- Nuns vow themselves to perpetual chastity and residence in a cloister.
- Princess Euphrosyne was a nun.
- Marrying a princess would legitimize Michael's hold on power.

The third of those was not, historically speaking, *true*, because this was the Byzantine court, and legitimate power was generally a matter of opinion. It is not a matter of opinion, however, that Euphrosyne did indeed leave her convent, and she and Michael were married in 823 or 824.

Unfortunately for you, we have no idea how Michael pulled it off. Euphrosyne was a princess locked behind convent walls, and then she was an empress. That is the sum total of what our sources say. Not so good for finding out how you can pull off the same feat . . . *great* for Michael's reputation. Because he probably succeeded by paying off the abbess. I mean, he donated money to the convent. A *donation*.

Some rescue.

☸ THE HAPPILY EVER AFTER

Byzantium gets a happily ever after?

Euphrosyne never returned to the convent where she had been exiled for two decades. Michael reigned for around nine years, with her at his side the entire time. The royal couple had no children, so there was no second son to scheme a way to inherit the throne instead of the emperor's only son from his earlier marriage, Theophilos. In fact, the three family members seem to have gotten along well. Euphrosyne probably helped arrange her stepson's marriage to a provincial noblewoman, Theodora, which would never have happened without his father's approval.

Michael died in 829, at nearly sixty years old, and Theophilos inherited the throne peacefully.

Really.

Theophilos reigned for nearly thirteen years before falling sick and dying in the palace. Theodora was at his side the entire time. When her husband died, Theodora took over de facto rule as regent and became one of the most powerful women in Byzantine history.

You wanted guidance for how to save a princess? Well, Michael II was accused of treason, was imprisoned and nearly murdered, beat the charge, murdered the emperor instead, seized the throne, started a royal dynasty, *and* saved the princess.

Not bad for a country kid with a disability.

The PRINCESS SAVES HERSELF

ou're this far into your quest, and you haven't started longing for your *beautiful* and *idyllic* village? You haven't wished that no mysterious stranger had ever encouraged you to claim your destiny to fight the forces of evil? Remember the part where Satan taught you how to read, and John of Morigny tried to tell you that not being pursued by supernatural hordes of evil was better than being able to read? Good thing you disagreed, because right now it's 1489 and you're standing in Regensburg, earning some much-needed money as an abused servant to the owner of a printshop. You've definitely been getting a little restless, so it's good that you've formulated a way to revise your quest based on a hot tip in a printed tabloid pamphlet. Kunigunde of Austria, the daughter of the Holy Roman emperor, and her husband have been the subject of steamy gossip since her birth in 1465. Two years ago, Kunigunde married Duke Albrecht of Bavaria. That pamphlet has sounded the alarm about the duke's nefarious intentions. Looks like the job for a hero: you've got a princess to save.

✿ ON THE MARRIAGE OF PRINCESSES

Fun fact: when he married his princess, Michael II had it easy. All he had to do was stage one coup and suppress a few more. Much of the time, no European princess could ever find her Prince Charming for one simple reason: incest.

Marrying off children for political advantages was a great strategy for the medieval elite. The exchange of dowries and reverse dowries could be financially lucrative. But it wasn't a free-for-all. In the early Middle Ages, the western Church laid down strict rules about which degrees of genetic relationship counted as incest in God's (or what the Church claimed were God's) eyes. Cheating on those rules was of course rampant, especially because it gave both the families and the Church an excuse to declare an annulment if the marriage ever became politically undesirable. Nevertheless, by the tenth century, the royal families of Europe were running out of equally royal options for their sons and daughters.

This was fine for the prince, who brought his spouse into his own family and kept his rank. It was not so fine for the princess, who had to join her new family. Kunigunde was the emperor's only surviving daughter and one of the most valuable brides in Europe—and she had no choice but to marry down.

But for this particular princess, the inevitable demotion that came with marriage was the least of her problems.

❦ ON THE MARRIAGE OF KUNIGUNDE

Everything—and every*one*—had seemed respectable enough in 1486. The emperor and imperial government were having problems with Venice, Hungary, Bohemia, Switzerland, the lower nobility, the upper nobility, the Church, and the Ottomans. (In other words: business as usual.) Kunigunde was safe from all these conflicts at the court of her father's cousin, Duke Siegmund of Austria and Tyrol. (The Holy Roman Empire in 1486 was shaped vaguely like an egg with some yolk running down into Italy, and Tyrol was the yolk.)

Duke Albrecht of Bavaria had secured the emperor's permission to marry the princess. Bavaria was one of the empire's most politically and territorially powerful principalities, and Albrecht was busy making it even more powerful—he was a good choice. Siegmund had secured the emperor's permission to negotiate her dowry and other financial matters, and he was good at his job. By early December, the preparations were complete. On January 2, 1487, the princess wed the duke with her father very much not

161

in attendance, and afterward, new duchess Kunigunde moved to Munich with her husband. Respectable enough. Mostly.

But you snitched a copy of the tabloid called *The Conquest of Regensburg*, and you know the awful truth behind this fairy tale.

👑 ON THE STEALING OF KUNIGUNDE

The author of *Conquest*, whose decision to remain anonymous was surely for their own safety, insists that Albrecht stole the princess from her father, from the Holy Roman Empire, and from Christianity itself. The emperor had arranged for Kunigunde to marry the Ottoman sultan. The marriage would seal a deal to protect the empire from the eastern threat and lead to Kunigunde's successful conversion of the Turks to Christianity. (One can dream.) Albrecht had *forged* the letter giving permission for him to marry Kunigunde. It's representative of the way Albrecht stole the allegiance of Regensburg, seized control of the powerful city's government, and increased taxes on monasteries.

Never you mind that by the pamphlet's publication in 1489, Kunigunde and Albrecht already had two little daughters, the first of their eight children. Never you mind that they had hosted Kunigunde's brother—heir to the empire—for a congenial visit. And never you mind that the tabloid could more accurately be titled *The Decision of the Regensburg City Council to Give Most Control to Albrecht in Exchange for Money, and I Don't Like the Person Albrecht Appointed as Mayor.*

Never mind any of that. You're the hero. Albrecht was an evil duke. Kunigunde was a princess in dire need of a rescue. You get to save her.

👑 ON THE SAVING OF KUNIGUNDE

Unfortunately for you, Kunigunde had her own ideas about a rescue. Namely, that she didn't need it.

She had spent her childhood in the snake pit of the imperial court, occasionally mediating between supplicants and her father. As duchess, she forced her older son to accept the younger brother she favored as his coduke. Most important, she knew treachery when she saw it. Even when others failed to. And she had the power and intelligence to reveal it.

In the early 1500s, say the sources, all of Augsburg was entranced by a young prophet who had clearly rolled an eighteen in charisma. Anna Laminit was around eighteen years old and living in a homeless shelter when God chose her to be a saint on Earth. He did so by allowing her to survive without eating any food at all. And allowing her to flaunt her self-starvation. And, of course, allowing the people of Augsburg to throw money at her because of it.

Emperor Maximilian—Kunigunde's brother—sought advice from Laminit in 1502. Empress Bianca Maria Sforza organized religious rituals at Laminit's urging in 1503. Laminit earned even more money, a larger house, the seat of honor at church, and a secret affair with at least one member of the city's aristocracy.

Skip ahead to Munich, 1512. The widowed Kunigunde was watching Laminit profit from her "sainthood," and Kunigunde was having none of it.

The duchess invited, or "invited," Laminit to the convent that she had made her pious final home. Laminit made excuses. Kunigunde snorted and played travel agent. She organized Laminit's trip to Munich and convinced the Augsburg city council to let their star leave. In short, she gave Laminit no way to refuse.

The sisters at Kunigunde's convent greeted Laminit with much fanfare and the luxury of her own bedroom.

Kunigunde had prepared the room especially for Laminit. Not with decorations but with small holes in the door. She spied from behind the door as the visitor hid a bag of expensive fruit and pastries under her bed. Kunigunde watched as Laminit ate into her secret stash of food. Laminit was *finished*. But the duchess wasn't. Kunigunde waited patiently, then watched as Laminit threw her excrement out the window.

And that is the story of how an old woman and some gingerbread cakes unmasked a con artist whose decade-long scam had captured the minds, souls, and purses of tens of thousands. She finished a long, skill-

163

ful, and overwhelmingly successful career by succeeding where an emperor and an entire city had failed.

Princesses in medieval Europe needed rescuing. Albrecht may have been the craftily evil duke you read about in your pamphlet, and Kunigunde may have needed rescuing even more desperately than most. But unfortunately for heroes, sometimes the princess saves herself.

HOW *to* STEAL *the* CROWN

ou slew a dragon, sure. But have you tried slaying a metaphor?

Whatever coups you've witnessed and princesses you haven't rescued and minor wrinkles you've faced during your quest, you probably think you're in great shape to finally steal the throne and drive evil out of the kingdom forever ("forever" being a subjective term . . . very subjective). Your victories mean it's time for one more wrinkle. In medieval Europe, stealing the crown sometimes meant stealing *a* crown. The object.

On the plus side, crowns in general were rather popular jewelry among the elite of the elite. Philippa of Hainaut had ten different ones; Edward II of England had to use several of his crowns as collateral for loans. But other crowns held true power. Some countries had a designated crown (or crowns) that were necessary for coronation rituals. Even the legal heir could lose the throne to a different person who had been crowned with the royal regalia.

In the Middle Ages, Hungary was one of those countries, with the kingdom perpetually investing its future in the Crown of St. Stephen. This custom was not initially a problem for King Albrecht II and Queen Elisabeth. It wasn't even immediately a problem when Albrecht died in late 1439, leaving behind no male heirs but also the Polish and Hungarian nobility just itching to win the throne for themselves. Elisabeth, who was pregnant and desperately hoping for a son, simply took the official crown from the royal treasury to protect it from conniving noblemen. She hid it in her own chamber, in a case disguised as a bench.

The trouble started when the room—and thus the bench—caught on fire.

Elisabeth's most trusted lady-in-waiting, Helene Kottanner, managed to put out the fire. But the incident made the queen and her closest confidants nervous enough to move the crown from the queen's chamber back to the treasury. And right after that, Elisabeth received warning that some Polish nobles planned to steal the throne by forcing her to remarry. She fled without a second thought, without her jewelry, without her chambermaids, and, most important, without the Crown of St. Stephen.

What Elisabeth did have was the fervent hope of delivering an infant son who would need the crown to become king. She turned to Kottanner for the riskiest of favors: sneak back into the castle and steal . . . her jewelry. Her jewelry? Elisabeth was the daughter of the Holy Roman emperor and queen of multiple nations. Surely she didn't need . . . But Elisabeth insisted.

Terrified for her life—as she herself wrote in her account of events—but ever loyal, Kottanner agreed to go back for the jewels. Hiding the treasure under her dress, she smuggled the pieces out of the castle. She did not buckle one bit under the interrogation of the nobleman who tried to stop her: "Helene Kottanner, what is it you are bringing?" "I am bringing my clothes." The practice at misdirection would serve her well, because it turned out the jewelry heist was just a warm-up.

And that is how, on the night of February 20, 1440, Helene Kottanner and two helpers found themselves breaking into the vault of the royal treasury of Hungary to steal a crown. They wore black clothing to blend into the dark and felt shoes to muffle their footsteps. The men smuggled files and hammers underneath their coats as they made their way to the outermost of three doors protecting the vault.

Kottanner distracted the guards (or, as she puts it, God allowed them to be distracted) while the men filed, hammered, and *burned* their way into the most protected place in the entire castle. The party quickly realized they had forgotten two things. First, the empty place where the crown would be missing was extremely conspicuous. Second, the crown would not exactly fit under a coat.

166

Kottanner isn't entirely clear in her account who accomplished what, but the following things happened:

- the used files were thrown down the toilet
- the crown was smuggled, unnoticed, to the castle's chapel, which was dedicated to *Saint* Elisabeth of Hungary (1207–1231)
- the shelf on which the crown had stood was also smuggled out of the vault, so the crown's absence would be less conspicuous
- the vault doors' locks were replaced

The heist continued as Kottanner and her helpers stole a red velvet pillow from the chapel, pulled out some of the feather stuffing, and sewed the official state crown of Hungary inside.

But before they could get the pillow out of the castle—I am still not making this up—an old servant approached Kottanner to ask what this strange casing in front of the queen's old chamber's stove might be. Kottanner quickly sent the woman off to her own quarters to fetch her possessions, promising the other woman a prime position in the queen's retinue if she cooperated—and then burned the casing down to ash.

And then they had to make their escape across the frozen Danube. Really.

It was all worth it, though, because Elisabeth gave birth to a healthy baby boy, the future king of Hungary, who was sealed in his role by the Crown of St. Stephen.

If you're looking for a story of ice and fire to help you turn metaphor into reality, here it is. Any princess can save herself and wear a crown. In 1440, this princess and her lady-in-waiting stole the crown and saved a kingdom.

REAPING

YOUR

REWARD

HOW *to* WIN *the* PRINCESS

eroic quests end in one of two ways: death or success. Heroes themselves also tend to end up one of two ways: either a burned-out husk of a human being or married. You probably don't need instructions for the first option. But on the off chance you prefer marriage to a life mired in perpetual trauma, it's time to talk about how to turn saving the princess into winning her heart.

🌸 ISABEL

If you're really lucky, your quest did the hard work already. Well, if you're lucky and you're the greatest knight who ever lived. That was how some people remembered English warrior William Marshal (1146/47–1219). William was skillful (and lucky) enough not to die in battle, comfortable enough to ingratiate himself with a series of English royals, and successful enough at both aspects of knighthood to do *better* than winning the princess. King Henry II of England hoped his own daughters would be queens or German empresses, and oversaw their marriages accordingly. As for his most prized champion? Henry promised landless William the hand (and huge tracts of land) of Isabel of Stringuil, possibly the richest woman in the British Isles, and his heir Richard eventually honored that promise. Not a bad deal.

So, if you're in England, winning the princess after your quest would seem to have only one further requirement: be a noble.

Score: Be a noble; 1.

But who's to say you're in England? (Besides the setting of every heroic quest before yours.) You know perfectly well that if William Marshal had attempted the same cascade of good fortune in the Byzantine Empire, its royal court would have eaten him alive (possibly literally). And if you want to win the princess, it's better to learn from the worst-case scenario. So have a nice trip to Constantinople, and don't worry if you're bad with names. You'll only have to learn three or four this time.

❦ EUPHROSYNE, ANOTHER EUPHROSYNE, MARIA, AND ANOTHER MARIA

Remember how Byzantine court politics do not mess around? Remember the last Irene, Maria, Euphrosyne, Irene, and Michael? Fast-forward about 450 years and five more Emperor Michaels, add three Mongol factions and Bulgaria to the mix, and recall the exact same names you learned when you were saving the princess. This time, you're in 1259 and the future Michael VIII stands poised to steal the throne.

You might say Michael (1223–1282) and William Marshal took similar paths toward winning the princess. Both of them acquitted themselves well in battle and politics, and occasionally fought on the side *against* the ruler. Both of them married women who were symbolically, rather than genetically, princesses.

But only Michael regained the emperor's good graces, married his beloved grandniece, fell back out of the emperor's good graces, fought on the side of the Mongols for two years, returned to Constantinople and staged a coup, and turned his marriage into the foundation of one of the most successful dynasties in imperial history. William, on the other hand, had some land. So if you want to win a sequel as well as a princess, Michael should be your go-to example.

Like his long-ago, princess-*saving* predecessor Michael II, Michael VIII staged a coup in 1259 and executed the regent ruling in place of the young emperor. Unlike his predecessor, Michael VIII then blinded and exiled the child ruler in 1261, eliminating him as a future threat to the throne.

Michael accomplished a few minor things as emperor, such as recon-

171

quering Constantinople from the Latin west, restoring the Byzantine Empire, and spearheading a cultural and intellectual revival. His feats become even more impressive when you realize that Greek Byzantium was smack in the middle of the overly ambitious Italian city-states to the west, the Mamluks to the south, the Bulgarian Empire to the north, and above all, the Mongols to the south and east.

Two of those Mongol states were as hungry as ever. The Golden Horde utterly ravaged Hungary in 1241 and was eager for a second round; the Ilkhanate destroyed Baghdad in 1258. Byzantine geography was not ideal.

Luckily, the Mongols were quite happy to manage their relationship with Byzantium through marriage alliances—a process Michael knew intimately, having been married to a former emperor's grandniece. His daughter Euphrosyne headed off to marry unofficial khan, or leader, Nogaj of (most of) the Golden Horde, and little Maria was sent to Abaqa Khan of the Ilkhanate.

(You've only just arrived in Byzantium, and already Michael, Nogaj, and Abaqa have won their princesses! Imagine what's going to happen when the story continues.)

These arrangements suited Maria and Euphrosyne just fine. Khans could marry as many wives as they wanted, but Mongol queens generally held more formal power than western noblewomen. In the Golden Horde, Euphrosyne managed to secure a Greek name for her daughter, and chose (because why not) Euphrosyne. We'll call her Euphrosyne 2. Hold that thought.

Meanwhile, Maria grew up in the Ilkhanate and learned how to manipulate Byzantine *and* Mongol rulers. Under her influence, Abaqa protected and aided the Ilkhanate's Christians to the extent that Maria was even attributed with performing miracles.

And no, she wasn't done yet. After Abaqa died in 1282, Maria's widowhood got off to a bad start when she was essentially forced to marry her stepson. Eventually, she—shall we say—*exiled herself without permission* back to Constantinople.

Score: Be a noble, 2; be a prince, 1; be a Mongol prince, 2.

Now-emperor Andronikos II, Maria's brother, might have intended to use her to secure yet another alliance. One way or another, Maria wouldn't let him dream of it. She founded and entered the wealthy monastery of St. Mary of the Mongols—in honor of the Virgin Mary, but also in honor of the people and nation she considered hers.

Instead, Andronikos sent his daughter Simondis to Serbia. We'll leave Serbia, Simondis, her husband Stefan, and the letter S at that, and move on.

You'll recall that Andronikos's sister Maria had married the khan of one Mongol khanate, the Ilkhanate. Andronikos's sister Euphrosyne had married a major general of another khanate, the Golden Horde, and was khan-in-all-but-title of most of it. That title and the rest of the Golden Horde belonged to Toqta—who was as ambitious as Nogaj was powerful. Andronikos recognized this situation, and sent another of his daughters (also named Maria, because why not?) to marry Toqta. We'll call her Maria 2.

Score: Be a noble, 2; be a prince, 1; be a Mongol prince, 3.

❦ IRENE, IRENE, MARIA, AND MARIA

Michael VIII's daughter Irene did not marry nearly as well as her sisters, despite initial appearances. The Bulgarian Empire was Byzantium's "one that got away," and even Michael couldn't get it back through military force or marriage.

During Bulgaria's internal turmoil in 1257, the Byzantine emperor had sheltered the runaway Bulgarian ex-ruler Mitso Asen in exchange for a base of operations on the Black Sea's northern coast (a strategic position both politically and economically). In 1278, Michael made his big effort. He arranged Irene's marriage to the exiled ruler's son Ivan Asen III, and sent them off to Bulgaria with an army. It worked.

Score: Be a noble, 2; be a prince, 2; be a Mongol prince, 3.

On the other hand.

An ambitiously cold-blooded (or cold-bloodedly ambitious) Bulgarian noble, George Terter, was married to a woman named Maria (we're up to Maria 3) and even had an heir, Theodor.

George figured out that Michael needed his army everywhere besides Bulgaria, and maneuvered himself closer to the Bulgarian throne by marrying Ivan Asen's sister, also named Maria, because why not (this would be Maria 4). In 1279, he sent Maria 3 and Theodor off to Constantinople to prove his loyalty to Michael.

Score: Be a noble, 3; be a prince, 2; be a Mongol prince, 3.

But why be a loyal underling when you can be an equal? George seized Bulgaria for himself in 1280 and sent Ivan Asen and Irene running back to Constantinople.

Michael, who had secured a détente or an alliance with almost (almost) everyone else, did not attack Bulgaria. But George still understood that his political position was balanced on the edge of a knife, and bided his time.

Michael died in 1282. His son Andronikos II became solo emperor without major violence, because this is not Bulgaria.

Back in Bulgaria, George decided to take advantage of what was still the turmoil around Andronikos's elevation to reigning alone. He divorced Maria 4 and sent her to Constantinople, brought Maria 3 home from Constantinople, and was eventually able to negotiate back Theodor, too.

This new situation suited Theodor well. He reigned as co-emperor and learned a few lessons about how to hold on to power amid restless nobles. More importantly, he learned a few lessons about what *not* to do.

So, it's 1282. To recap:

- Byzantine Emperor Michael VIII has died peacefully.
- Andronikos II, Michael's son, has inherited the throne peacefully and is now emperor.
- Maria 1, Michael's daughter, has married the khan of the Mongol Ilkhanate, founded a monastery, and is currently off-screen.

- Euphrosyne 1, Michael's daughter, had married the military leader/khan who de facto ruled one faction of the Mongol Golden Horde, Nogaj.
- Euphrosyne 2 is the daughter of Euphrosyne 1 and Nogaj.
- Irene, Michael's daughter, was empress of Bulgaria, but has now become a high-powered Byzantine aristocrat. Good for her.
- George Terter was a Bulgarian noble with ambitions.
- Maria 3 and Theodor, George's wife and son, have been exiled to Byzantium but are now back in Bulgaria.
- Maria 4 was Irene's sister-in-law and George's second wife, but she is now in Byzantium.
- George Terter is emperor of Bulgaria.
- Theodor, his son, is co-emperor of Bulgaria.
- Back in England, William Marshal married an heiress and owned some land.

Meanwhile—remember Princess Irene, daughter of an emperor, who was a queen for less than a year before she had to run away to save her life? In 1341, Irene's granddaughter, also named (because *why not*) Irene, married even better. Forget Bulgaria. Irene 2's marriage made her empress . . . of the entire Byzantine Empire.

Sometimes you save the princess, and sometimes the princess saves herself. Sometimes you win the princess, and sometimes you have to let the princess win you instead.

But what if nobody wants to be won?

HOW *to* BE MARRIED *to the* PRINCE

o, you have to marry the prince.

This is good news for you, and not just if you're in love with him. Sure, the only way women can be heroes when married is some awkward retconning later. But what do heroes specialize in, if not breaking the rules? All you need is the right guide to help you have your prince and be a hero, too.

❦ OPTION 1: ANSELM OF CANTERBURY

Okay, yes, technically Anselm (d. 1109) was male.

Okay, yes, technically Anselm was a monk and also the archbishop of Canterbury.

And yes, technically, in the Middle Ages men could not marry men and monks could not marry at all, even if they were one of the most powerful bishops in the Church and one of the most important theologians of the whole Middle Ages. Allegorically speaking, though . . .

Writers and theologians in the Middle Ages loved allegory. That might mean personifying an abstract idea, like depicting Pride as a beautiful woman wearing too much makeup. Or it could mean envisioning a mundane story as an extended metaphor for a deeper truth. Like, *for example*, treating marriage as an allegory for Christ's love for his Bride—the human soul.

As you can imagine, monks and nuns who vowed their lives to celibacy and to Christ really, really appreciated this allegory. Twelfth-century monk Bernard of Clairvaux used it as the underlying theme of more than eighty sermons. Thirteenth-century mystic Mechthild of Magdeburg used it to write some wonderfully spicy poetry.

But slotting Christ's title as Prince of Peace into the bridal allegory is a little bit too cute and much too simplistic for a hero, which is where Anselm comes in. Our celibate friend lived a little before the Bride of Christ identity became all the rage, but well within the era of the man crush.

From surviving sources, it's impossible to tell whether any specific case included the "what happens in the monastic cell, stays in the monastic cell" DLC. But you might well think of the core element as brotherhood, fellowship, or the same kind of romantic friendship that medieval women nurture. Still envisioning medieval warriors as the embodiment of raw masculinity? Well, actually, because men in the Middle Ages felt less threatened by women, it was much more acceptable for them to display lavish emotions like romantic love for each other.

Look no further than Anselm's letter to fellow monk Brother Gilbert: "The gifts of your affection, dearest friend, are dear to me. But they can never console my heart, deprived of you in my longing for your beloved person . . . Indeed, it will never be consoled for its separation except by recovering its other half, my sundered soul . . . Never having experienced your absence, I did not know how sweet it was for me to be with you, how bitter without you."[13]

Not only was Anselm willing to write these words, he also would have known they would be read aloud, and not just to or by Gilbert. He would have assumed his letter would be preserved for later generations to read. In other words, the archbishop of Canterbury had a man crush, and everyone around him thought it was completely normal. So sure, you might not *marry*-marry the prince. But your bond of love could be just as deep.

Of course, not everyone can be the archbishop of Canterbury. Some of us have to settle for infuriating the archbishop of York.

Twice.

---

13 Letter 84, Walter Fröhlich, trans., *The Letters of St. Anselm of Canterbury* (Cistercian Publications, 1990), 1:219.

Strictly speaking, Margery Burnham Kempe (d. after 1438) greatly annoyed the archbishop of York, the mayor of Leicester, some residents of Bristol, some priests in York, pilgrims in Jerusalem, pilgrims in Spain, her husband (they made up), and her son (they made up, too). At least, so she wrote in the collection of stories where she chronicles her spiritual life, which included plenty of external adventures to ground it. And unlike John of Morigny (the monk who accidentally had Satan teach you to read), *The Book of Margery Kempe* is completely a Christian text in which its author recounts multiple visions of Christ. But she's the perfect guide for *any* heroine who has to be married to the prince while continuing to be a hero.

Most medieval women who can be called "badass" were nuns or prophets, widows taking over their husband's authority, or queens seizing power on behalf of their sons. And Kempe is no exception. She was indeed committed to her family. She gave birth to fourteen children, convinced her husband to have a celibate marriage rather than leaving him, nursed him when he got too old and sick to take care of himself, and raised at least one daughter who was as adventurous as her mom. Kempe even brought her husband along on some of her own adventures. But the *Book* shows a married woman who lived her life on her own terms.

Kempe could not sit still. Despite her obvious wealth, she attempted to start two different businesses. They both failed, which doesn't speak well to her skills as a businesswoman but says a lot about her drive. After an agonizing and bleak postpartum period following the birth of her first child, though, she dedicated her life to a religious quest of sorts to, more or less, marry Christ (spiritually) while still married (humanly) to her husband. At the heart of her quest were two common phenomena: pilgrimage and education.

The hero is in the details, though. Kempe's multiple pilgrimages took her to Canterbury—and Jerusalem, Rome, Germany, and Spain. She was one of the most impressive world travelers in all of medieval Europe. She wasn't quiet and demure about it, either—her loud displays of religious

178

devotion and scolding her fellow travelers made a lot of people grouchy, and she sure acted like she didn't care.

As for education?

Kempe read (or had someone read to her) some of the most popular and acceptable religious texts of her day. She learned them well enough to model her life after saints like Katherine of Alexandria, the one who outwitted fifty philosophers, and Birgitta of Sweden, who advised popes. More outstandingly, though, she apparently studied the Bible firsthand— enough to quote verses in her own stressful debates. But the Middle Ages sometimes had difficulty accepting smart women. Kempe was detained on suspicion of heresy multiple times. However, she knew both the Bible and Christian theology well enough to talk her way out of it. Again, multiple times. Sure, Kempe wasn't wielding a sword or fireball. But given that the English Church's persecution of heretics was in full flame in Kempe's day, she had all the quick, witty remarks any hero would dream of having.

So if you thought the travel part of your quest was just great and being *asked* to quest on behalf of someone else was annoying, make like Margery Kempe: the ordinary woman who broke all the rules of female decorum to be loud, smart, and definitely not heretical.

✿ BUT FIRST . . .

Contrary to all stretches of the human imagination, married people in the Middle Ages could fall in love without committing adultery and go on adventures that had nothing to do with saving their children. Sure, part of you might still want to be like Arwa, the last queen of Sulayhid dynasty Yemen. She literally went to war—army versus army—to prevent one of her suitors from reaching her palace.

But even she ultimately gave in to marriage. At least on parchment, without them ever living together. Arwa understood that sometimes being married to the prince is necessary, and it does not have to mean the death of your heroics. Furthermore, Arwa and her *fifty-four years* of independent rule as queen regnant of Yemen in her own right offer you a fitting role model for a reason even beyond her immense diplomatic skill and military ruthlessness.

According to Yemeni chroniclers, the beautiful Arwa was most definitely *not* thin—quite the opposite. And after you attend the feast to celebrate your quest and eventual marriage, you won't be, either.

HOW *to* FEAST
LIKE *a* KING

 laying dragons makes you a hero. It also makes you hungry. A roasted pig with an apple in its mouth? That's sidekick's play. If you want to keep up with the Savoys, your pig needs to have an oil-soaked cotton rag stuffed in its mouth. Then you have to set the rag on fire so the pig will breathe flames. Also, the pig needs to be covered in gold.

Thus it went at the court of Amadeus VIII of Savoy in 1420. With Philip the Good of Burgundy in 1454, on the other hand, four-and-twenty blackbirds might have sufficed for a quiet, private breakfast. For a feast, you needed to bake eight-and-twenty musicians in that pie. Alive musicians, mind you.

Besides "wouldn't the fire melt the gold" (no, because the "gold" was often raw egg yolks smeared all over the pig), two points in these examples merit attention. First, good thing Amadeus wasn't alive to witness how thoroughly he had been outclassed. Second, since the musicians in the pie are alive and playing far better music than your bard, what are you supposed to *eat*?

Philip's five-day feast at Lille in Burgundy has you covered. In between watching its jousts and skits, you could munch on veal-brain ravioli and ruin your teeth with exotic fruits made entirely of even more exotic sugar. And who could turn down faux eggs and onions made of sugar?

But don't just spend the next five days committing the sin of gluttony. As a hero, you're *possibly* going to marry the princess but *definitely* going to receive a massive reward of money, land, political power, and the need to maintain that power through rituals like feasts. So pay attention, because soon the only dragon you'll be slaying is your culinary budget.

✿ 1. No, You Don't Have a Choice

No matter where or when in the Middle Ages you go, you're not getting out of this one. When Moroccan merchant Ibn Battuta (1304–1369) reached the town of Iwalata in the middle of the Saharan desert, ten days' travel from the nearest settlement in one direction and twenty-four days in the other, the villagers' immediate reaction was to lay out a ceremonial meal. The connection between feasting and power is even baked into the titles "lord" and "lady." The words derive from the Old English *hlaford* and *hlafdige*, or "loaf-ward" and "loaf-dough-maker."

If only medieval feasts were just a matter of throwing rolls and pretzels (a medieval invention) at your guests. Or a matter of carefully served lasagna (also a medieval invention) and a thousand florins' worth of embroidered decorations. Wherever and whenever you were in the Middle Ages, feasts of course were an assertion of the host's wealth and power. But then things got complicated, because feasts had a spread of other uses that did vary from culture to culture, and even feast to feast.

In early and high medieval Scandinavia, for example, feasts served as a way to reinforce the two-way bonds between host and guests. An invitation was a way to honor the guest; accepting an invitation signaled allegiance, alliance, or protection. By the thirteenth century, the parents of the bride and the groom competed to see who could invite the more prestigious guests to the wedding feast.

Or take those thousand florins spent on embroidery. That extravagance belonged to Holy Roman Empire ruler Maximilian I in 1500, when he hosted a masquerade in Munich—and nearly every thread and embroiderer's fee went to decorating costumes and scenery with imperial symbols. Everywhere guests looked, from swishing skirts to hanging tapestries, the extravagant splendor proclaimed that the name Maximilian was a synonym for the empire itself.

So pay close attention to your celebratory feast. You've got a lot of learning to do.

🏵 2. THE HALL IS NOT A HALLWAY

You've got a lot to worry about before you can start debating whether to use thread or glue to attach the 2,500 mirrors of various sizes to the deep blue fabric covering the entire hall ceiling in order to represent the planets, the constellations of the zodiac, and the full night sky. For one thing, the hall.

"The biggest room possible" is a good start, but it's not enough. In early medieval England, it might have been easy enough to, say, use "the entire interior of the biggest building in the settlement" and then fill it with tables. But it's 1475, and you're in Pesaro, Italy. That's where the five-day wedding feast of Costanzo Sforza and Camilla Marzano d'Aragona needed a hall with space for nine tables that could seat twelve people each. Plus there was room for an organ, a long table to display gold and silver treasures, more than one hundred servants and enough space to make sure they didn't trip over each other, an open performance area large enough to stage a ballet, and bleacher seating along the sides for people who were elite enough to watch the entertainment, but not elite enough to eat.

Because there was no such thing as over-the-top when it came to late medieval feasts, when the duke's palace in Burgundy did not have a sufficient space for a grand feast its planners envisioned in 1430, they built one.

The second absolute, no-exceptions requirement for a feast in Christian Europe was tablecloths. Costanzo and Camilla had all of the tables for their wedding feast freshly painted—some in gold—and then draped heavy white linen over them anyway. Tablecloths and napkins separated people from mere peasants, who ate off bare wood and wiped their fingers on their clothing. When you host your own feasts, you'll need to be sure you purchase entirely new tablecloths and napkins each time. To clarify, you will need to purchase multiple sets of napkins. Multiple sets per meal. 183 (But don't worry about what to do with them afterwards. If you head to fourteenth-century Paris, you'll find a *thriving* market for secondhand napkins.)

❦ 3. YOUR DECORATING BUDGET WILL BE OUT OF THIS WORLD

No matter how majestic your castle, its great hall can still look greater. You can't go wrong by covering the walls with multicolored tapestries of elaborate designs or mythical scenes—the classics never go out of style. The best feast-design committees (yes, committees) transported guests to another universe, like with Camilla and Costanzo's night sky ceiling-carpet. Their decorations also drew on the well of romance and imagination. The couple had their walls blanketed entirely with thick ornamental greenery (cut fresh for each day, naturally), evoking the literary role of forests as their own world of magic and mystery.

Table decorations blurred the lines between décor and entertainment and between décor and food. Small flowing fountains and ship sculptures might have sufficed for Charlemagne and his sons in the ninth century. (Fountains maintained their popularity, but not on tabletops. At Philip's 1454 "Feast of Pheasant," the fountain structure took the shape of a human woman, and guests could refill their glasses from the red and white wine pouring constantly from her . . . right.) But in fifteenth-century Italy, you couldn't even get away with a gold-covered pig belching fire. You needed gorgeous, exotic, *wildly expensive* peacocks with their tails grandly arrayed—and, yes, covered in gold—to spit the fire. Or models of castles and Crusader battles constructed out of wood and pastry dough.

Pro tip: Don't eat the castle. You don't want splinters.

❦ 4. INDIGESTION

The feast following the coronation of Queen Katherine in 1421 England (who had married one of the less deadly Henrys) featured only three courses. Don't sigh in relief. The third course alone consisted of dates covered in a syrup of powdered escargot and colored cream, roasted porpoise, fried prawns, lobster slathered in sauce, a dish of dates, prawns, red shrimp, great eels, roasted lamprey, white escargot, and a meat pie apparently decorated with four angels. One course did not mean one food.

Camilla and Costanzo's twelve courses start to seem a little more impressive now. Especially since they were so elaborate, the introduction to each course merited speeches by two characters dressed as Greek gods.

✿ 5. THE BURNING QUESTION OF WHAT TO DO WHILE YOU DIGEST

Early and high medieval Scandinavia kept it drunk and participatory. Poets—sometimes the lords themselves—sang epics and drinking songs. Late medieval Mali upped the game to multiple types of poets assigned specific types of praise and historical songs, plus ceremonial costumes often resembling animals.

By the time of Camilla and Costanzo's wedding in 1475, food was almost the least important part of a feast. (Hence guests coveting the bleacher seats, not just the wedding couple wanting to show off to as many people as possible.) In addition to the table centerpieces, you'll need to have skits and displays (hilariously known as "subtleties") at the end of each course, skits and displays between courses, entrance parades for the entire town to partake in, and events between the different meals of the feast.

Frequently, the tabletop Crusader battles were accompanied by men reenacting (the death- and defeat-less parts of) the battles in the performance area. Maybe it was 1454, and a high-ranking courtier dressed up in a white satin robe with a black coat to personify Lady Eglesia—the Church as a gorgeous woman. He (or she) was led into the hall riding on a giant mechanical elephant draped with silk. (Or so the courtier in question claimed in his *extensive* chronicle entry about the feast. The other chroniclers agree there was a Lady Eglesia and an elephant. Only the courtier claims he got to sit atop an elephant.)

In between the meals themselves, you'll have to stage footraces, jousts, and above all, dances. Get ready to move all those tables out of the way and then put them back. Multiple times. And, most important, be sure you have large vats of wine and that the ladies in attendance are wearing very long skirts.

Not for the reason you're thinking. (Well, that one, too.) In 1393, French king Charles VI hosted what is likely the most infamous feast in the entire Middle Ages, which featured a masquerade ball whose tragedy had nothing to do with assassinations by poison. As a joyful surprise to guests, a group of dancers dressed as wild men sprang into the hall and began running about as wild men do. Their costumes were covered in linen, then tar, and then shaggy flax, and it was nighttime, and all the light in the hall was supplied by torches.

The masquerade's name of *Bal des Ardents*—Ball of the Burning Men—tells you everything you need, but don't want, to know.

Four of the dancers died in agony. One survived by jumping into a vat of wine. The final one survived when a teenage onlooker rushed over and pushed him underneath her skirts. The dancer was the French king. Duchess Jeanne of Berry was the only person brave enough to try to save him and smart enough to succeed.

(Be like Jeanne, not Charles.)

❦ 6. FEASTS WERE ALSO—ROLL WITH IT—FUN

The word "banquet" began life as an extra meal tagged onto a feast, usually hosted sometime late in the evening. Unlike other meals, banquets were served buffet-style. And, more important, they included serve-yourself wine in more than ample amounts. In the Islamic world, the equivalent of banquets was the only time alcohol was publicly served to those who wished to partake. Those who did also had the option to enjoy foods meant to slow the rate of intoxication so they could drink more.

Which is to say: the Middle Ages turned late-night drunk snacking into a formal meal.

Even if you prefer not to drink, you're going to have some great gossip for the next morning.

The WORLD
TURNED UPSIDE DOWN

he mysterious stranger thuds the book closed. Their eyes are bright. "What do you think?"

You trace the letters at the top of the cover, familiar from the carvings you see in religious art. D-E D-O-M-I-N-I-S D-R-A-C-O-N-U-M. "Um," you say, "actually I just meant the title."

The stranger blinks. "Oh," they say as the sun's first rays appear on the horizon. "It says *Concerning the Masters of Dragons*." They hold out the book. "It's for you."

So, patch your boots, grab your sword, and take one last look at your village. You've got dragons to slay.

ACKNOWLEDGMENTS

If this book occasionally reads like *A Fantasy Hero's Guide to Fifteenth-Century Germany and Tenth-Century Cairo*, it's a shining tribute to John Van Engen and Olivia Remie Constable, brilliant scholars and my mentors at Notre Dame. As fifteenth-century Germans would say, *ane sie laufft niht*.

But as for every author and every book, my "without whom, nothing" spans a group so large, thanking them all would require a book so long that even *my* dog couldn't eat it all at once. In particular, though: Mark Evans is somehow always there for me in exactly the way I need at that moment, and knows that always includes making me laugh. Although he would deny it, Pat Werda is the best listener I know. When I don't have the answers, I know I can always turn to Juan Sebastián Lewin.

Caitlin Smith, Anna Munroe, Bobby Derie, Johannes Breit, Roel Konijnendijk, Will Knight, Hunter Higgison, Adam Barr, Brad Groundwater, Cassidy Percoco, C. D. Marmelle, Dan Howlett, Dominic Webb, Fraser Raeburn, Hannah Friedman, J Porter, JaShong King, Jenn Binis, Jeremy Salkeld, Jonathan Dean, Kyle Pittman, Lisa Baer-Tsarfati, Max MacPhee, Mike Siemon, Nathan Kasimer, Rob Weir, Ruairi McGowan-Smith, Sarah Gilbert, Sihong Lin, Simon Lam, Stefan Aguirre Quiroga, Thomas Lobitz, Tim Byron, Travis Warlow, Tyler Alderson, and Xavier Cortes have been to Scarborough Fair and back with me far more often than they deserve. Ron James has shown me the beautiful and terrible power of storytelling that is the soul of all histories. Through his wisdom and friendship, he reminds me every day why I do this.

The library staff at Saint Louis University and the University of

Notre Dame have worked miracles for me in obtaining sources that otherwise might as well have been lost in dusty codices for all time. My parents, Jeffrey and Kathleen, continue to slay my own dragons so I will never have to. The soundtracks to *Civilization VI* and *Europa Universalis IV* have never let me down.

I had somehow never realized that "writing a book" involves a lot more than the writing part. Ronnie Alvarado, my editor, has walked me through this painful realization while somehow knowing my writing better than I do. Bruno Solís is no illustrator; he's an artist and an inspiration. Patrick Sullivan and Jenny Chung clearly used some pretty strong *maleficium* to turn my little Word document into an actual book.

Most of all, though, not a single word of *How to Slay a Dragon* would exist without the entire AskHistorians community—flairs, inquirers, readers, and above all, my fellow moderators. As Mechthild of Magdeburg would say (in thirteenth-century Germany this time), they shine into my soul like the sun against gold.

SELECTED SOURCES

In addition to the translators and authors cited below, I am indebted to a long list of scholars whose research lies beneath so much of *How to Slay a Dragon*. They include, but are by no means limited to, John Van Engen, Dan Hobbins, Claire Jones, Olivia Remie Constable, Brad Gregory, Hildegund Müller, Paul Acker, Anna Akasoy, Judith Bennett, Karl Bihlmeyer, Renate Blumenfeld-Kosinski, Albrecht Classen, Karin Graf, Monica Green, Ulrich Haarmann, Barbara Hanawalt, Lars Ivar Hansen and Bjornar Olsen, Geraldine Heng, Tamar Herzig, Kathryn Kerby-Fulton, Nehemia Levtzion and Jay Spaulding, Kathleen Llewellyn, Bernd Moeller, Tom Shippey, Gerald Strauss, and Werner Williams-Krapp.

1. Bailey, Michael. "From Sorcery to Witchcraft: Clerical Conceptions of Magic in the Later Middle Ages." *Speculum* 76, no. 4 (2001): 960–90.

2. de la Brocquière, Bertrandon. *Le Voyage d'Outremer de Bertrandon de la Broquière*, ed. C. H. Schefer (E. Leroux, 1892), 22.

3. El Daly, Okasha. *Egyptology: The Missing Millennium: Ancient Egypt in Medieval Arabic Writings*. UCL Press, 2005.

4. Fanger, Claire. *Rewriting Magic: An Exegesis of the Visionary Autobiography of a Fourteenth-Century French Monk*. The Pennsylvania State University Press, 2015.

5. Fröhlich, Walter., trans. and comm. *The Letters of St. Anselm of Canterbury*. 3 vols. Cistercian Publications, 1990.

6. Haarmann, Ulrich. Introduction to *Das Pyramidenbuch des Abu Ga'far al-Idrisi*. Franz Steiner Verlag, 1991, 1–94.

7. Heller, Sarah-Grace. "Angevin-Sicilian Sumptuary Statutes of the 1290s: Fashion in the Thirteenth-Century Mediterranean." *Medieval Clothing and Textiles* 11, edited by Robin Netherton and Gale R. Owen Crocker (2015): 79–97.

8. Mulder-Bakker, Anneke B. *The Dedicated Spiritual Life of Upper Rhine Noblewomen: A Study and Translation of a Fourteenth-Century Spiritual Biography of Gertrude Rickeldey of Ortenberg and Heilke of Staufenberg.* Brepols, 2017.

9. Radner, Joan N., trans. *Fragmentary Annals of Ireland.* University College Cork CELT Project. 2004, 2008. https://celt.ucc.ie/published/T100017.html.

10. Riley, Henry Thomas, ed. *Munimenta Gildhallae Londoniensis.* 3 vols. Longman, Green, Longman, and Roberts, 1860.

11. ———, ed. and trans. *Memorials of London and London Life in the XIIIth, XIVth, and XVth Centuries: Being a Series of Extracts, Local, Social, and Political, from the Early Archives of the City of London.* Longmans.

12. Smith, Martyn. "Pyramids in the Medieval Islamic Landscape: Perceptions and Narratives." *Journal of the American Research Center in Egypt* 43 (2007): 1–14.

13. Tlusty, B. Ann, ed. and trans. *Augsburg During the Reformation Era: An Anthology of Sources.* Hackett Publishing Company, 2012.

FURTHER READING

1. Bennett, Judith. *Ale, Beer, and Brewsters in England: Women's Work in a Changing World, 1300–1600*. Oxford University Press, 1996.

2. Brink, Stefan, with Neil Price. *The Viking World*. Routledge, 2008.

3. Constable, Olivia Remie. *Housing the Stranger in the Mediterranean World: Lodging, Trade, and Travel in Late Antiquity and the Middle Ages*. Cambridge University Press, 2004.

4. Corfis, Ivy A., and Michael Wolfe. *The Medieval City under Siege*. Boydell & Brewer, 1999.

5. Cortese, Delia, and Simoneta Calderini. *Women and the Fatimids in the World of Islam*. Edinburgh University Press, 2006.

6. Daston, Lorraine, and Katherine Park. *Wonders and the Order of Nature, 1150–1750*. Zone Books, 1998.

7. Freedman, Paul. *Out of the East: Spices and the Medieval Imagination*. Yale University Press, 2009.

8. Herrin, Judith. *Women in Purple: Rulers of Medieval Byzantium*. Princeton University Press, 2001.

9. Madigan, Kevin. *Medieval Christianity*. Yale University Press, 2015.

10. Magnusson, Roberta. *Water Technology in the Middle Ages: Cities, Monasteries, and Waterworks after the Roman Empire*. Johns Hopkins University Press, 2001.

11. *Medieval West Africa: Views from Arab Scholars and Merchants*, edited and translated by Nehemia Levtzion and Jay Spaulding. Marcus Wiener Publishers, 2003.

12. Naswallah, Nawal. *Annals of the Caliphs' Kitchens: Ibn Sayyar al-Warraq's Tenth-Century Baghdadi Cookbook*. Brill, 2007.

13. *A Renaissance Wedding: The Celebrations at Pesaro for the Marriage of Costanzo Sforza and Camilla Marzano d'Aragona, 26–30 May 1475*, edited and translated by Jane Bridgeman with Alan Griffiths. Brepols, 2013.

14. Sumption, Jonathan. *Pilgrimage: An Image of Medieval Religion*. Faber and Faber, 2002.

15. Truitt, E. R. *Medieval Robots: Mechanism, Magic, Nature, and Art*. University of Pennsylvania Press, 2015.

FURTHER READING

ABOUT THE AUTHOR

Cait Stevenson earned her PhD in medieval history from the University of Notre Dame. She concentrates on breaking down the barriers and hierarchy among academic and popular history. As sunagainstgold, she moderates AskHistorians, the internet's largest public history forum, where she also writes on topics ranging from medieval inheritance laws to whether seventeenth-century children playing with toy guns said their equivalent of "pew, pew, pew." She is proud to live and work in St. Louis, Missouri.